Mastering Cone 6 Glazes

Improving Durability, Fit and Aesthetics

John Hesselberth and Ron Roy

foreword by Janet Mansfield

ECHO POINT BOOKS & MEDIA, LLC
Brattleboro, Vermont

A word about our copyright: Please respect it and allow us to be compensated for the thousands of hours and thousands of dollars we invested of our own resources to bring this book to life. If a person wants to use the information in this book, including the glazes, we ask only that they buy a copy of the book and refrain from passing the information around by other means. A percentage of any money we earn from this book will go into continuing research on glazes. Thanks for honoring this simple request.

No part of this book may be reproduced, digitized, stored in a retrieval system or transmitted in any form or by any means (this includes, but is not limited to, microfilming, photocopying, scanning and retyping) without the written permission of the copyright owners except by a reviewer who may quote brief passages in a review.

Registered trademarks included in this book are the property of their respective owners and not of the authors.

The authors welcome feedback and suggestions for future work and may be contacted through their publishing company or, more directly, through their web site at www.masteringglazes.com/

Echo Point Books and Media would like to thank Shari Zabriskie for her suggestion to republish *Mastering Cone 6 Glazes*.

Published by Echo Point Books & Media
Brattleboro, Vermont
www.EchoPointBooks.com

All rights reserved.
Neither this work nor any portions thereof may be reproduced, stored in a retrieval system, or transmitted in any capacity without written permission from the publisher.

Copyright © 2002, 2020 by Ron Roy and John Hesselberth

Mastering Cone 6 Glazes
ISBN: 978-1-63561-885-3 (paperback)

Cover design by Alicia Brown
Cover photograph by H. Mark Weidman of sake jar by Ron Roy

Contents

FOREWORD 7
PREFACE 9
ACKNOWLEDGMENTS 10
A NOTE ABOUT SAFETY 11

1 13
INTRODUCTION 13
Why This Book Is Needed 13
What Do We Mean by Stable or Durable Glazes? Is That Different from "Food Safe" Glazes? 14
The Seger Unity Formula and Its Relevance to Our Work 19
Conclusions 21

2 23
BASICS OF GLAZING AND FIRING 23
Safety First 23
Purchase and Storage of Glaze Chemicals 23
Weighing and Mixing 24
Glaze Suspension (Flocculents and Deflocculents) 28
Bisque Preparation 30
    Bisque Firing 30
    Cleaning 31
    Glaze Resists 31
Applying Glazes 32
Firing 34
    Loading 34
    Rate of Firing and Cooling 35
Summary 35

3 37
TESTING GLAZES FOR STABILITY AND FIT 37
Testing for Resistance to Acids 38
    In-Studio Testing 39
    Quantitative Testing by a Professional Testing Laboratory 40
    Interpretation of Results 40

Testing for Resistance to Alkalis 43
Testing for Resistance to Thermal Shock (Clay/Glaze Fit)...........44
Testing for Resistance to Knife Marking 46
Testing for Wear and Scratch Resistance 46
Testing for Chipping Resistance..47
Testing for Suitability for Use in a Microwave Oven 47
Summary 49

4 51
MAKING A STABLE GLAZE..51
Rule 1. Have Enough Silica 52
Rule 2. Have Enough Alumina 53
Rule 3. Thoroughly Melt the Glaze..54
Rule 4. Use Moderate Levels of Colorants and Opacifiers 55
Guidelines for Improving Glaze Stability 58
    Guideline 1 58
    Guideline 2 59
    Guideline 3 59
What about Limit Formulas? 59
Summary 60

5 61
FITTING GLAZES TO YOUR CLAY BODY 61
Understanding Crazing, Dunting and Shivering 61
    Crazing 61
    Shivering or Dunting 62
Determining Clay/Glaze Fit for Your Materials.............................62
Understanding Dilatometer Measurements...................................63
Expansion Test Glazes and How to Use Them 67
Interpreting Calculated and Measured Expansion Numbers.........69
Are Calculated Expansion Numbers Useful? 70
Expansion Test Glazes 72
Summary 81

6 83
STONEWARE AND PORCELAIN GLAZES 83
Base Glazes 86
    High Calcium Matte/Semimatte Glazes 86
    General Purpose Glossy Base Glazes 92
    Glossy Base Glaze 2.. 96
    A Clear, Glossy Liner Glaze 97
    A Zinc Semimatte/Glossy Base Glaze 98

Specialty Glazes 102
    A Chrome/Tin Pink Glossy Glaze 102
    Waxwing Brown... 104
    Waterfall Brown 106
    A Cone 6 "Maiolica" Glaze 108
    Alumina and Magnesia Matte Glazes 110
Summary 110

7 111
DEVELOPING YOUR OWN GLAZES 111
Glossy versus Matte 111
Level of Transparency/Opacity 112
Solid Color versus Variegated Glazes 112
Ron's Approach to Glaze Development 113
John's Approach to Glaze Development 116
Summary 118

Bibliography........................119

Glossary 121

Postscript............................128

Appendices........................129

A 130
RECOMMENDED MATERIALS..130

B 133
THE SEGER UNITY FORMULA 133
Background 133
A Simple Example 134
The Computer's Role in Glaze Formulation............................136

C 138
PROGRAMS FOR GLAZE CALCULATION.......................138

D 141
TESTING LABORATORIES FOR GLAZES 141

E 143
FIRING CYCLES FOR ELECTRIC KILNS 143

F 145
MATERIALS ANALYSES 145

G 153
GLAZES USED FOR DEVELOPMENT OF RULES 153
    Rule 1 (Have Enough Silica) 153
    Rule 2 (Have Enough Alumina) 155
    Rule 3 (Thoroughly Melt the Glaze) 158
    Rule 4 (Use Moderate Levels of Colorants or Opacifiers) ... 158

H 159
USEFUL REFERENCES FOR LEACHING DATA 159

I 162
LIMIT FORMULAS FOR CONE 6 GLAZES 162

Index 163

FOREWORD

Research into glaze and glaze technology is one of the most absorbing activities associated with the art of ceramics. I can remember intense periods of my ceramic research, working with a small test kiln, preparing tests and firing them, opening the kiln the following morning, and repeating the procedure again that day. This activity would go on for many weeks as I built up my understanding of the properties of the materials that were available to me at that time. On one particular occasion, vanadium oxide and its uses in promoting texture in an earthenware glaze was the object of the research; on another it was the increasing percentage of calcium carbonate in a stoneware glaze to simulate a marble-like surface. Such concentration can be rewarding. In this enlightened book by John Hesselberth and Ron Roy, both well known for their knowledgeable and practical approach to ceramic chemistry, we are offered the benefit of their concentrated research into cone 6 glazes, an area of ceramics that is becoming increasingly popular. The principles used in their studies, however, could be applied to glazes at all temperatures. Their stringent criteria set new standards for the whole profession and fully meet their aims in assisting potters to make "durable, trouble-free, reliable and reproducible" glazes. Their work is original, honed by experiment and tested thoroughly. Importantly, it is accessible, readable and straightforward. Theirs is a disciplined stance and they urge potters to be equally disciplined, not taking a random approach but to understand each step they take and why they are taking them.

Mastering Cone 6 Glazes is published at a time when there is a need for skills. Potters need to be able to realise their ideas through an understanding of the materials and processes of their art. Potters looking for reliable and stable glazes will find information that is forthright and clear, the reasoning sound and presented in a language that all potters can understand. And there is a challenge too: potters and their suppliers of materials and equipment need to be socially and professionally responsible for their output production. Potters should ensure that their work meets reliable and high standards and suppliers should offer analyses of materials that are correct and repeatable. Safety is an important aspect of making and selling pottery and the authors take this seriously, especially the leaching of toxic materials and the ability of the potters' wares to resist use and abuse; however, the authors are not alarmist but practical, offering common sense solutions to the storage of materials, the handling of chemicals and the making of work that will stand the test of time.

Dipping into the text of Mastering Glazes I found myself reading on for some time, discovering many useful facts, for example: the crazing, dunting and shivering of glazes is explained clearly; why some pots after use for cooking in the microwave are hotter to the touch than others; and how the presence of one material affects another during firing at certain temperatures. The authors give us a choice of methodology in many instances. They present options for different ways of tackling a problem depending on a potter's individual preference and interpretation.

This book is designed to be a continuing thesis. The authors welcome readers' comments and results of further experimentation, and they hope that the text will be augmented regularly so that the knowledge presented will be a vital and worthwhile contribution to the available literature on glaze chemistry in a format that is accessible to all involved in the field of contemporary ceramics. Working with this text will provide the potter with a manual for professional practice and give long-term pleasure and satisfaction.

Janet Mansfield
Potter/ Publisher of Ceramics: Art and Perception & Ceramics TECHNICAL

PREFACE

This is a book written by potters for potters. While we will deal with some difficult technical issues, we will try to do it in plain language that most potters understand. In some cases this may mean that we oversimplify and offend the more highly technically trained person. If we do, so be it. Our purpose is to write a book that will help potters make better, more stable or durable functional glazes. We have chosen to write in a style and using words that are commonly used by studio potters and ceramic art teachers; however, we have also included a Glossary to further aid in understanding.

We believe this book is desperately needed by studio potters who make functional pottery. It may also be of significant help to those who make sculptural or decorative work and who want to be sure their work will still look the same after a few years (or centuries) as it does when it comes out of their kiln. We present information that is not available in any other published form and, unfortunately, is not taught in very many college-level ceramics programs. It is also very much a "work in progress". While we have drawn on the published literature where possible, we have done our own research to extend our knowledge of how to make durable glazes. We welcome suggestions on how to improve the material herein and are continuing our own studies in this general area.

With those few words, we welcome you to the world of more stable, durable Cone 6 glazes—glazes that, while being suitable for use on functional pottery, are also extremely attractive.

Ron and John, January 2002

Where to Buy This Book:

In Canada: Glaze Master Press, 15084 Little Lake Road, Brighton, Ontario K0K 1H0

In the United States: Frog Pond Pottery, P.O. Box 88, Pocopson, PA 19366

On the internet: www.masteringglazes.com

From your local pottery supply store

From our publisher: www.echopointbooks.com

ACKNOWLEDGMENTS

There are many people, without whom, this book would never have seen the light of day. First and foremost are our spouses Lucy Roy and Judy Hesselberth. We would have been lost without their continuous support.

The origin of the book has to be attributed to the Clayart computer forum. That is where we first met and it was through that forum that we came to realize that there was both a need and a desire on the part of many potters to have a book of this type. We also received much needed support and encouragement from our many friends on Clayart, some of whom we have never met.

We are particularly indebted to four very fine potters who proofread and critiqued this manuscript. They are Heidi Haugen, Craig Martell, Liz Willoughby and Phil Yordy. Their comments were immensely helpful in improving the accuracy, readability and clarity of what we have written. They have also been enthusiastic supporters and coaches.

Many thanks to all who made suggestions and brought errors to our attention for the second printing - a special thank you to Jon Singer for his extensive suggestions.

Brandywine Science Center and Alfred Analytical Laboratory gave us timely and accurate measurement of the leaching of materials from our glaze candidates. Without their help we would not have been able to develop the understanding needed to write this book.

We are grateful to Rob Lockhart of Rampart Lion Communications who gave us excellent advice on printer selection and on numerous typography and layout questions.

Joyce Hesselberth and David Plunkert of Spur Design provided an excellent cover design and Mark Weidman made an outstanding photograph of the sake jar we chose to put on the cover.

Thank you all!

A NOTE ABOUT SAFETY

While many glaze chemicals are no more dangerous than powdered rocks, others are toxic and must be handled with great care. Sometimes the danger comes from inhalation of dust or fumes; sometimes it comes from ingestion or absorption through tissue. Since there is a lot of available information regarding the safe handling of glaze chemicals we will not try to duplicate that information in this book. It is the responsibility of each person using the information in this book to make sure he/she knows how to handle glaze chemicals safely! Get Material Safety Data Sheets (MSDS) for every chemical you buy or use. Read them. Understand them. Follow the recommendations on those sheets. Learn and use good personal protection and housekeeping practices. You must take responsibility for your own safety and the safety of people around you.

While the glaze information and recipes presented in this book are believed accurate and durable respectively, each potter must take responsibility for his or her own products. There is variability in raw materials, mixing and application techniques, and firing conditions over which the authors have no control. In addition, glazes are sometimes affected strongly by the clays, slips, underglazes and/or coloring oxides which are used with them. Make sure you test any glaze on every combination of the above that you use—what is good on one combination can be a disaster on another. All of the above factors can affect the final product and each potter must test that final product to assure suitability for use.

"By the term 'glaze,' we understand in general every superficial coating on clay ware covering either the whole surface or a part of it, which is intended either to prevent the absorption of liquids and gases, or to serve as a decoration, or as a ground layer on which to apply the painting in colors, enamels or metals. These superficial coatings are always and inseparably connected with the idea of a ceramic product, of being fixed by a fire process on to a clay body which is the carrier of the glaze....A glaze can therefore always be defined as 'a more or less glassy coating' whose ingredients are either melted to a vitrified slag or porcelain-like mass (as in dull glazes) or to a glass or enamel (as in the clear and opaque glazes)."

The Collected Writings of Hermann Augustus Seger

1
INTRODUCTION

Why This Book Is Needed

This is a book about glazes—reliable, stable/durable glazes that can be used on stoneware and porcelain. The book is intended for use by independent studio potters, teachers and others who want a readily available source of thoroughly tested glazes that will perform reliably. We will also explain the principles of making durable glazes so readers can formulate their own glazes with more confidence. Why do we believe this is necessary? What new contribution will this book make to the literature where dozens of books about glazes already exist? These are easy questions to answer. It is an unfortunate fact that there are thousands of glaze recipes circulating among potters or printed in books that, for one reason or another, are totally unsuitable for use on functional pottery and may even be of questionable durability for less demanding sculptural or decorative work. Unfortunately, many of these unsatisfactory glazes are being used on functional pottery. The reasons they are unsuitable vary and they include: 1) a lack of reliability due to glaze ingredients that are notoriously inconsistent in composition, 2) a lack of stability or durability to the point that the coloring oxides leach out over time or the glaze surface easily cracks, chips, accumulates metal marks or becomes dulled after repeated dish washing, 3) a glaze surface that is pitted, pinholed or crazed so badly that it is not easily cleaned or maintained after each use and 4) glazes that are so ill-fitting that they shiver and leave sharp splinters of glaze ready to injure the user of the pot. While shivering is not a frequent problem at Cone 6 the related problem of dunting is quite common. We must be alert for it and pay particular attention to clay/glaze fit.

Many of these unsuitable glazes may once have been labeled as not for use with food or more generally for use on functional pottery; however, that disclaimer has often been lost over time. More often the durability question has not been addressed. Because of the lack of available information on durability, this book will add an important dimension to the available glaze literature. Many glaze developers do not recognize that it is almost impossible to tell by visual examination whether or not the glaze is likely to be durable. They assume that if it looks like "good glass" it will be durable. In fact, a significant amount of testing is required to determine durability and, while some of that testing can be done by a potter in her own studio, some requires complex analytical laboratory testing equipment. Only recently has the sophisticated portion of the testing become available at prices potters can afford.

It is also a sad (in the authors' view) fact of life that today many schools of art, where future potters are trained, do not give students a good foundation in glaze chemistry and formulation. Whether this is because it is considered unimportant or because the faculty does not have the skill or time or funding to teach the subject undoubtedly varies from institution to institution. All academic institutions should not be painted with the same brush, however. There are some schools that do give students a good foundation in what might be called the craftsmanship side of becoming a potter. Still, all in all, the trend in recent years has been to de-emphasize craftsmanship for the artistic or design side of pottery in academic institutions.

So the need is real. There are many studio potters around the world who will benefit from having a source of stable glazes. We will attempt to present this information in simple, straightforward terms. We cannot, however, completely avoid explaining some of the technology that applies to glaze formulation. Where we need to get into the technology, we will do our best to keep those discussions as free from "techno-speak" as possible.

What Do We Mean by Stable or Durable Glazes? Is That Different from "Food Safe" Glazes?

Glazed ceramic pots have been used to contain food for thousands of years. With the exception of glazes containing one material—lead—there have been no documented instances of anyone having been harmed by materials leaching from a ceramic glaze. Note that the preceding sentence does not prove that no one has been harmed, but only that if people are being harmed it is in such small numbers that documentation has not been possible. In North America, and indeed in most of the world, only lead and two other materials—cadmium and occasionally barium—have been proven or are thought to be toxic enough that their use in ceramic glazes should be regulated. In the United States the Food and Drug Administration (FDA) requires potters who use lead and cadmium to assure they release no more than specified amounts of those materials during a 24 hour room temperature leaching with 4% acetic acid. This test has been designed to assure that pottery passing the test will not result in ingestion of significant levels of lead or cadmium. Within the U.S., California has a labeling requirement for lead-containing glazes that is more stringent than those of the FDA. In Canada, the government requires similar testing. In North America, there are no other product-related regulatory requirements a potter must meet to make and sell pottery for use with food.

In one sense, then, (the regulatory sense) the term "food-safe" can be used for all ceramic glazes which contain neither lead nor cadmium or which meet the required leaching test standards for those materials. Indeed, it would seem from an analysis of the glazes some glaze formulators or authors are specifying as "food safe" that this is the definition they have used. We believe the time has come to hold ourselves to a higher standard: we believe we should use glazes that are as stable as possible and leach only tiny amounts, if any measurable amount at all, of glaze components into food and beverages. We understand that there are potters who believe this is unnecessary nonsense. They apparently believe that the amounts of glaze components that leach into food, even from a very unstable glaze, are not a safety concern and amount to nothing more than a minor food supplement. We believe potters are not in the food supplement business and that our customers are entitled to have durable and attractive glazes on the pottery we sell. Making durable glazes is an integral part of good craftsmanship. We also know that, even if there is no safety issue, certain glaze materials (e.g. copper) can impart a bad or bitter taste to food. This is a surprise we do not want to give to customers. We also know from testing that some very attractive glazes are so unstable that you can draw the color right out of them with a few minutes or hours exposure to weak acids like vinegar or lemon juice. Wouldn't it be better to use stable glazes on plates or other functional pottery or even on tiles that might be put on a kitchen counter or exposed in an outdoor installation to acid rain? Do you want your pottery to look the same after several years as it did when it was new? Would stable or unstable glazes be more likely to result in a customer buying more pottery from you?

See Figures 1-1 through 1-3 for an illustration of this kind of instability. The glazes used for this demonstration are very attractive semimatte

Figure 1-1. These saucers were glazed with glazes whose recipes appear in well-known books. They were fired to Cone 6.

Figure 1-2. The juicy slices of lemon were left on the saucers for about 2 hours, and then the saucers were rinsed and dried.

Figure 1-3. The color has completely and permanently been drawn out of the saucers by the lemon juice. These saucers are ruined!

glazes found in books by well-regarded authors. There is no comment in either book about the durability of the glazes. The saucers were exposed to lemon juice for about two hours. While these saucers were glazed from recipes found in books, we could also show you commercial glazes that behave just as badly. These are premixed glazes sold to studio potters and are labeled as being "food safe".

Our purpose in this book is to show you how to avoid making glazes that behave like these do. We will come back to one of these glazes later in this chapter and illustrate why it has such poor performance.

At the other end of the spectrum, with regard to "food safe" glazes, are those who believe glazes should be virtually inert. They believe the term "food safe" should be used only for glazes containing no materials which might conceivably cause harm or for glazes so stable they have truly superior leaching performance. These people would propose that glazes leach less, in the standard leaching test, than would be allowed as a contaminant in drinking water. There are no data to support this position—it is only an opinion; however, it does make more complex the use of the term "food safe".

In fact, the primary problem with using the term "food safe" is that there is no agreed upon definition and no definitive research to back up the definitions at either end of the spectrum. If we were to use the term we would have to define it thus creating controversy with those who think it should be defined some other way or, as some authors do, use the term without defining it and hope no one asks. We don't believe either of these approaches is appropriate.

For the above reasons we will, for the most part, not use the term "food safe". We do, however, believe the glazes contained herein are safe to use with food provided the clay/glaze fit issues described later in this book are also addressed. In fact, our glazes are far more inert than most people believe is required. Most, but not all, will even meet the most extreme proposed use of the term as explained above. We have leach tested all our base glazes in a standard way so you can get some idea of their relative stability. We also provide various reference points (Appendix H) which will help you, the potter, decide for yourself what standards or goals, if any, you will work toward in the glazes you put on dinnerware. Among these reference points are 1) the lead and cadmium standards in the U.S. and California (those must be followed if you use these materials—as explained below, you will not find them in any recipe in this book) and 2) the U.S. drinking water standards for materials likely to be used in glazes. A reference is also given to Recommended Daily Allowances, if any, for materials likely to be used in glazes. This is not to suggest that any of these numbers be applied or used as "standards," but only to give a relative indication of the toxicity of various materials and/or their importance in the human diet. In the end, each potter has to make up her own mind how to handle this issue. All we can provide is information and an approach to make glazes as stable as we know how.

Rather than "food safe", we have elected to use two other terms to describe the glazes contained within this book. It should be pointed out that these two terms are far more demanding and all-encompassing terms than "food safe"—at least compared to the way that term is used today. They are more demanding because they not only require that the glaze leach minimal amounts of materials in a standard leaching test, but also that the glaze meet other criteria to show that it is suitable for use on functional pottery. These criteria are things such as craze resistance, durability in a dishwasher or on exposure to other alkaline materials and resistance to marking by silverware or metal serving utensils.

The first of these other terms is a **liner glaze.** By our definition, a liner glaze is one that is very durable in use (to be defined later) and contains no materials where leaching into food might be considered a problem. For example, these glazes may contain zirconium, titanium or tin-based whiteners as well as iron oxide as a colorant; however, they will stay away from other colorants such as nickel, chromium, cobalt and copper. We both favor using this type of glaze for the most rigorous types of service: namely on the inside of vessels meant to contain large amounts of liquid or those that might be used in the oven, e.g. pitchers and casserole dishes. You may, of course, decide to use only liner glazes on the insides of all your functional pottery; some potters are taking this approach. Doing this will limit your color palette to whites, tans and browns. You may also decide to add color, other than from the brown family, to these glazes and use them on non-food-bearing surfaces.

The second category of glazes presented we call **durable or stable glazes** (and we will use those words interchangeably). These glazes will contain materials that could cause concern if they were to leach in significant quantities; however, they have all been tested for leaching and were found to be near the stable end of the spectrum of glazes. In addition, they leach less of these materials than found in some commercially available glazes that are labeled "food safe". In all cases the results of our leaching tests are included so you can make up your own mind whether to put them on food or other functional surfaces. These stable/durable glazes are glazes that we would use on small cups, bowls, plates and the like. Of course they would also be suitable for vases, flowerpots, lotion bottles and other pots which are not likely to be used for food, but which will see hard use. We also highly recommend you consider using them even when the durability requirements for your pottery seem less stringent. Who can tell when a vase might be used as a sake decanter or what bird droppings might do to an outdoor tile mural? Many times our pottery ends up being exposed to a much harsher environment than we had imagined.

All this said, there are still some materials we have elected not to use in the glazes in this book or to use only under very restricted circumstances. These materials have some level of controversy around them regarding their use on functional pottery; although we have been able to find little or no data to show that they have caused specific problems. The controversy may result from concerns about their toxicity (e.g. barium) or from such properties as their tendency to cause nonuniformities or instabilities (e.g. large amounts of lithium supplied to the glaze as lithium carbonate) which can result in unpredictable glaze properties. Generally, there are safer or less controversial substitutes available for these materials. We should point out, though, that stable/durable glazes certainly can be made using these materials and our omitting them in no way reflects a recommendation on our part that they be banned from food surfaces or functional pottery in general. We are simply trying to provide a set of reliable, durable, attractive glazes that potters can use with minimal or no concern and, after some initial testing on their own to confirm our results, use without an expensive ongoing testing program.

In addition, as you may have guessed, we have not used recipes containing lead or cadmium. There is little or no need for lead at Cone 6 or above. Cadmium's only redeeming feature is that it can give oranges and reds difficult or impossible to achieve by other means. In both cases, however, we believe the burden placed on the potter who uses either of these materials will result in more cost, concern and red tape than the average studio potter or teacher will be able to bear. In addition, most studio potters do not have the expertise or the equipment required to safely handle these materials and most schools do not either.

The Seger Unity Formula and Its Relevance to Our Work

We will try to minimize the use of technical terms and complicated technology-based explanations in this book. We understand that many potters do not have a strong foundation in ceramic science. However there is one concept, or way of describing a glaze, we feel is an essential tool to meaningful discussion or illustration of stability and durability. We believe all potters who mix or formulate their own glazes should have some familiarity with a system that allows comparison of the composition of one glaze versus another. In a subsequent chapter we will provide some standards of comparison for stable glazes. For potters the most commonly used system is the Seger molar formula for describing a glaze, now usually called the unity molecular formula, the Seger unity formula or just the unity formula. In the late 1800s, Hermann A. Seger, the father of modern glaze chemistry, developed a way of describing a glaze that allowed easy and meaningful comparison with other glaze formulas. It also provided a way to group glazes into classes or types of glazes, e.g. by firing temperature or by compositional characteristics. That method is so useful and has become so universally used in the ceramic glaze research literature and in other books that we all should make ourselves familiar with it. At the same time, there are those who feel that looking at the percentages of the components of a glaze is a better way to examine a glaze. While we have no argument with those who prefer to look at molar percentages—that is just another way of presenting the same information that is in the unity formula—most of the common glaze calculation programs calculate only weight percentages. This is beginning to change. At least two glaze programs calculate both weight and molar percentages. Weight percentages usually do not give useful information when it comes to comparing composition of two glazes or to determining glaze stability. Another advantage of using the Seger formula is that it provides a simple and standard way of looking at the fired glaze instead of looking at the input materials. While we recognize these differences of opinion on how best to think about the composition of a glaze, we have chosen to use the Seger unity formula to describe glaze compositions throughout this book.

Let's take a slight detour to illustrate how the Seger unity formula helps in predicting and understanding the stability of a glaze. Table 1-1 shows both the recipe and the unity formula for the Jade Green glaze (the saucer on the right shown in Figure 1-3).

Jade Green, Cones 4-6

Glaze Recipe		Unity Formula	
Potash Feldspar	40.0	Fluxes	
Barium Carbonate	20.0	K_2O	0.127
Gerstley Borate	10.0	Na_2O	0.080
Zinc Oxide	9.9	CaO	0.138
EPK	10.1	MgO	0.041
Silica	10.0	Li_2O	
Add:		ZnO	0.336
Copper Carbonate	5.25	BaO	0.278
Comments:		Stabilizers	
1. Original recipe called for colemanite instead of Gerstley Borate.		Al_2O_3	0.295
		B_2O_3	0.157
		Glass Formers	
2. This is a very unstable glaze. DO NOT USE FOR ANY FUNCTIONAL WORK		SiO_2	2.011
		Si:Al	6.5

Table 1-1. Recipe and Seger Unity Formula for Jade Green Glaze shown in Figures 1-1 through 1-3.

Note that the recipe on the left side of Table 1-1 shows us how to mix the glaze, but it tells us nothing of the composition. You will learn, however, in Chapter 4 that the silica (SiO_2) level of 2.011 shown on the right hand side of this table violates the first "rule" of making stable glazes and indicates instantly that this glaze is very likely to be unstable.

If you are interested in learning how to calculate the Seger unity formula there is a short summary of it in Appendix B. More detailed descriptions can be found in the published literature (Hamer and Hamer under "Calculation" or Rhodes <u>Clay and Glazes</u> under "Calculating Glazes"). You will find that you will become more familiar and comfortable with interpreting Seger unity numbers just by reading and using the material in this book.

While we believe you should be familiar with the fundamentals of the Seger unity formula approach, there certainly is no need to calculate the numbers by hand. Several computer programs are available to do the calculations. We provide a list of those which we are aware of at press time in Appendix C. If you are going to formulate your own glazes or test published recipes we highly recommend getting one of these programs.

Material Analysis Accuracy Is Critical. A special warning is needed with respect to using glaze calculation programs or doing manual calculations: Make sure you use real, and not theoretical, analyses for your materials. Some books and some glaze calculation programs have used theoretical or outdated analyses which result in very different numbers. Always ask your supplier for up-to-date material analyses for the materials you use and modify the material database in your glaze calculation program to match the specific materials you are using. Material composition varies from time-to-time and place-to-place and your results will be much more predictable with current, accurate materials analyses. For even more reliable information note the lot number from your materials bag and contact the manufacturer or mine directly. Not all suppliers consistently update their own files of material analyses. The material analyses shown in Appendix F are mine-approved and current at time of publication of this book.

Describing glaze composition in molecular terms was only one of Seger's many contributions. For example, he also invented pyrometric cones and made many contributions to the manufacture of bricks and roofing tiles.

Conclusions

We hope you are convinced that the need for this book is real. Formulating stable or durable glazes is not difficult. It is also a fact that **Cone 6 glazes can be both durable and attractive.** Very little compromise of aesthetic choice is necessary to have durable glazes that will perform well in use. If you don't believe that, take just a moment to peek at the glazes we have developed for this book (Chapter 6). While we feel you will agree that we have developed some very attractive glazes, we consider those to be only departure points to help you do your own glaze formulation.

We believe the material that follows will help you formulate your own durable **and** attractive glazes.

"It is sometimes held by artist potters, especially in England, that it is a waste of time to calculate glazes according to the Seger formula.... In spite of these objections, the pioneer potter would be unwise to deprive himself of this useful tool...which only involves simple arithmetic.... There are so many possible causes of failure in a potter's life that it would be a mistake for him to reject a method which saves valuable time, which is certainly capable of enhancing both the technical and the artistic merits of his glazes, and which in the process may possibly also enlarge the confines of his wits."

Michael Cardew, Pioneer Pottery

2
BASICS OF GLAZING AND FIRING

Safety First

Safety considerations have to be given high priority when handling, mixing and firing glazes. There are four primary considerations to address: 1) protection from dust during mixing of glazes and handling of dry, unfired glazes, 2) toxicity of the materials themselves, 3) control of fumes during firing and 4) proper disposal of excess materials. As mentioned in the Preface there are several sources of information on this subject and we will not duplicate that information here with one exception. During the process of mixing and applying glazes perhaps the most important safety issue is use of a good dust mask. Remember that silica fines stay suspended in air almost indefinitely and will be present long after you have finished weighing and mixing your glazes.

Do not buy one of the dust masks available at the typical hardware store. These are intended to protect only against "nuisance dusts", i.e. dusts you might encounter when mowing your yard or sanding a piece of wood. The particle size of these dusts is significantly larger than those we deal with as potters. Silica, clay and other finely powdered ingredients will go right through these "nuisance dust" masks. Instead, invest about $50 in a good dust mask with a P100 rating (removes 99.97% of 0.3 micron particles), along with several extra filters. A series of two articles in *Clay Times* (Rossol, Nov/Dec 1999 and Jan/Feb 2000) gives an excellent description of how to properly fit and use a mask as well as a thorough discussion of how to select the right mask for your use. Go for the best; your lungs are worth it! High quality protective equipment of the type mentioned is available from industrial supply houses (Grainger Industrial Supply and Acklands Grainger are good examples in the U.S. and Canada respectively) or check your phone book under the heading of Safety Equipment. It is up to each of us to follow safe practices including wearing appropriate protective equipment, assuring adequate ventilation or air exchange and practicing good housekeeping in our studios, kiln rooms and associated work spaces.

Purchase and Storage of Glaze Chemicals

Always buy glaze materials in the largest quantity you can manage from the standpoint of cost and storage. Full 50-pound bags are ideal. If you are a sizeable production studio you might want to buy multiple bags. Not only will you have much less problem with changes in composition over time, but you also will save a lot of money. Buying 50 pounds is sometimes less expensive (total cost) than buying 25 pounds. You will also have fewer problems with the occasional labeling mistakes that occur in your supplier's hands. The fewer times a material is repackaged, the less chance mistakes will be made in labeling.

Proper storage requires that you keep glaze chemicals clean and dry. Remember also that some of the materials we use are toxic and should be kept out of the reach of children and pets. If you move your glaze materials

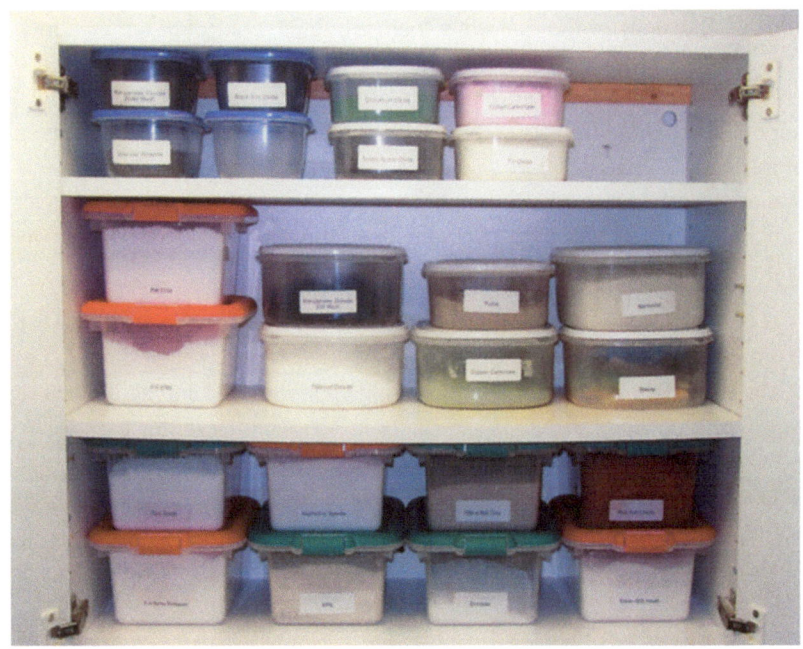

Figure 2-1. Chemicals kept in smaller amounts are stored in sealed plastic boxes with labels securely attached.

from their original bag, it is a good idea to tear off the label and put it in the new container. The authors use various plastic containers for storage. Part of John's glaze chemical storage is shown in Figures 2-1 and 2-2.

Weighing and Mixing

A good balance is the first requirement for accurate and reproducible glaze preparation, but you don't need to have extreme accuracy. An Ohaus triple beam balance with tare weight compensation is a good choice. This is the type of scale we use as shown in Figure 2-3. Never use a spring-type kitchen scale—they simply are not very accurate. Having the tare weight feature will allow you to use any convenient container to hold your materials while you weigh them. Depending on the batch size you plan to mix, you

> Note that the hanging weights used to increase capacity of a scale are stamped with their actual weight and make good calibration weights.

may also want additional 500 gram and 1000 gram weights to minimize the number of times you have to weigh out a single ingredient. There is one caution we would give about balances, however: many second hand and older balances have problems that can affect their precision or accuracy—see our recommendations in the sidebar on the next page for checking balances—this should be done on a regular basis.

For weighing out 200 gram test batches (the minimum we recommend for initial tests), accuracy to the nearest half gram is probably sufficient for most materials; although you will want to try to weigh minor components such as colorants to the nearest 0.1 gram.

Perhaps the most important consideration in weighing out ingredients is to make sure you don't get confused on how far down the list you are or, if you need multiple portions of the same ingredient, how many portions you have weighed out. Probably more glaze batches have been ruined from interruptions (like the telephone ringing) during the weighing process than from any other single cause. You must develop a system that will prevent this if you want reliable, reproducible results from your glaze formulation. An

Figure 2-2. Plastic bins sold for holding sorted recyclable materials make an ideal container for full bags of glaze materials.

Are you having difficulty accurately weighing out fractions of a gram? Try this. Weigh out one gram. Put it on a piece of paper and use a small spatula or similar tool to shape it into a "log". Then carefully subdivide the log into sections to get the amount you need.

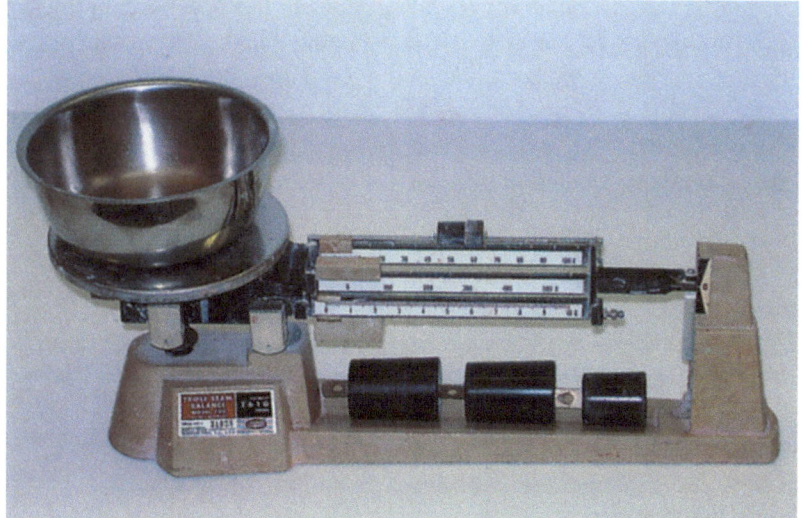

Figure 2-3. An Ohaus balance of the type useful for weighing out glaze materials.

excellent way to check yourself is to weigh the entire batch of dry materials before you add them to water.

The system we recommend is as follows: Check your balance and zero it before you start. Also check its accuracy with a known weight (see the notes in the sidebars for instructions). Spread out a large sheet of newspaper near where you will weigh your materials. As you weigh each material, place it in an individual pile on the newspaper and make a note of what it is and how much right on the paper next to the pile. If you have to fill your container more than once to get enough of a specific material, keep those piles separate from each other too. When you have finished weighing, double check the number of piles against your recipe to be sure everything is there in the right amount. Then, and only then, proceed to the mixing step.

Mixing glazes is best done by adding powder to water. There is a major difference between doing it this way and adding water to powder. But before you add any powder to water, dry blend all the ingredients together. This doesn't need to be a thorough blending process; it should be done by raising a minimum level of dust and with your mask still firmly in place on your face. What you are trying to avoid here are things like 1) having a material which does not suspend very well in water (like frits or nepheline syenite) hit the water first and form a "rock" on the bottom of your container or 2) globs of floating bentonite.

You will need approximately 90 milliliters of water per 100 grams of dry glaze mix. This will vary quite a bit depending on the specific materials you are using, but you can always dilute with more water as you go. Selecting the best amount of water to use is something of an art and we can only suggest a couple of "rules of thumb" on how to do this—here are some of the techniques we use:

1. One rule of thumb for adjusting water to the best level in a glaze slurry literally involves your thumb. Put your dry thumb into the slurry up to the first knuckle. Withdraw it and let the glaze drain off. If the glaze sticks to your skin in a continuous film, but peels away from your thumbnail, it is about the right consistency. Please don't ask whether or not nail polish affects this test. Neither of us uses it.

2. A paint viscometer (a small cup with a hole in the bottom you buy at a paint or hardware store) can also be used to adjust the water level in glazes. Better yet, make your own. Make a small cup, put a quarter inch hole in the bottom and attach a handle so you can dip it in glaze slurry easily. Fire it to maturity. Calibrate it by dipping it into and filling it with a glaze that seems about right. Time how long it takes to empty itself to within about one half inch from the bottom (if you let it go all the way to the bottom, the measurement will be less accurate). Adjust your other glazes to the same time.

> It's good practice to always zero your balance before each use. To do this, set the weights on the slide bars to zero. If you have a tare beam, put the pan you use on the balance. Slide the weight on the tare beam until the pointer points at "0". This can best be done one of two ways: 1) Bump the beam to get it swinging slowly up and down and adjust the weight on the tare beam so the pointer moves equal distances on either side of zero. 2) Adjust the weight on the tare beam so the pointer stops at zero, then gently tap the frame of the balance to be sure the pointer has not stopped off its true balance.

3. A third technique is to keep a supply of bisque shards. Dip one in a normal way and determine the glaze thickness by scratching through and visually checking the thickness (your magnifier will really help make this evaluation). Of the techniques discussed, this is probably the most accurate.

4. You can also make up glazes to a constant specific gravity; however do not use a hydrometer (floating "meters") to measure this. They are notoriously imprecise in glaze slurries. Instead, weigh an empty 100 ml graduated cylinder. Fill it with 100 ml of glaze slurry and weigh it again. The difference in weights divided by 100 is the specific gravity. Once you learn the desirable specific gravity for each glaze, you can adjust future batches to the correct number rather easily.

Adjustment of glazes to have the right amount of water comes primarily from experience; after a while you will know when the consistency is correct just by looking at the way the glaze moves when you stir it.

Now that you have the piles of dry glaze powder roughly blended into a homogeneous mix and the starting amount of water measured into an adequate size plastic pail, carefully and slowly pour the dry mix into the water. Do it gradually so that it doesn't accumulate into a big pile on top of the water. After it sits for a few minutes the powder should be completely wetted. Do not add additional water at this point; wait until it is mixed to best judge the consistency.

A good thorough blending is next on the agenda. You can use a mixer powered by an electric drill if you wish. However we find a brush, a simple paint stirrer, a spoon or just a plain stick of wood, depending on the size of the batch, are more than adequate to do the initial mixing. After stirring for a few minutes you are ready for sieving or screening. This is an important step and should not be omitted. We recommend sieving twice through an 80-mesh screen. After the first sieving, stir again for a couple of minutes to assure good intermixing of the materials. After the second sieving your glaze is ready to use. You may occasionally find a glaze material that needs finer sieving to get the desired uniformity, but 80 mesh is normally adequate.

Sieving deserves another word or two. For best results sieve your glazes, not only when they are first mixed, but also before every use. It is a rare glaze that will stay so uniformly dispersed that it can be evenly applied with only restirring. Either the flat, manual screens attached to the bottom of a plastic or metal dish or the Talisman style sieves will work: the choice between them is a matter of personal preference and available funds. If you use the flat screens you can force the glaze slurry through the screen with a brush. If you use your hands instead, be sure to wear rubber gloves. For small batches of 200 grams a stencil brush works well. For larger batches try a large stencil brush or a paintbrush that has been cut off to have about one inch long bristles.

> Oops, I got my glaze too thin. What do I do now?
>
> The easiest thing to do is to let it sit undisturbed for 24 hours. Then carefully skim clear water off the top of the bucket. Sponge out the last bit if you need to. Remix, rescreen and test again. Repeat if necessary.

Glaze Suspension (Flocculents and Deflocculents)

There is much confusion over how to solve problems such as 1) glazes that settle too rapidly, 2) glazes that don't "dry" quickly on the surface of bisque or 3) glazes that "dry" too quickly when they are being applied by brush thereby making even application impossible. Rather than explain these potential problems item by item, we will focus on explaining flocculation and deflocculation and recommend some products that work reliably. We would also point out that the following explanation is intended for those interested in solving their glaze suspension problems, not for those interested in the exact science of these phenomena. We will take some liberties to keep our explanation simple. There are, of course, solutions to these problems other than the ones we will recommend and if one of those is working for you, continue to use it.

The terms flocculation and deflocculation are among the most confusing we potters encounter. In fact, from reading the literature, it is clear that some authors have either been confused or have not been able to describe these phenomena clearly thereby adding to the difficulty of understanding them. In addition, most of the literature discussions pertain to managing casting slips instead of glazes. Simply stated, flocculation and deflocculation describe the physics of what is going on with particles suspended in water, but it may seem to mean the reverse of what one might conclude from visualizing the process.

It is important to recognize that a glaze suspension is composed of particles of varying size—some relatively big and shaped like irregular rocks or boulders (e.g. feldspars, frits, colorants) and some relatively tiny and shaped like small flat rocks or "skipping stones" (e.g. clay). If only "boulders" were present they would settle quickly and form a hard cake on the bottom of the container—potters sometimes call this hard-panning. If only the "small flat rocks" were present they would stay in suspension much longer although they too would eventually settle out. This is because the physics of the situation is such that these small clay particles are attracted to one another to form loose, open structures called flocs. Even when these flocs settle they form a much looser layer on the bottom of the container, which is more easily redispersed.

When both "boulders" and "small flat rocks" are present in the same suspension several things can happen. First, the physics can be such that the entire mixture is flocculated. That is when a number of the "small flat rocks" associate with or surround one or more "boulders" and the entire agglomerate stays in suspension fairly well. This is normally the case when the clay content of a glaze is 10% or higher. However, the entire mixture can also be deflocculated where the "boulders" settle out quickly and the "small flat rocks" stay in suspension by themselves. The difference is caused by the ionic and electrostatic nature of the materials dissolved in the water in which our glaze materials are suspended. Very small differences in composition can make large differences in the flocculation/deflocculation balance. Even the impurities (type and amount) in your tap water can upset this balance and is yet another reason why glaze recipes sometimes don't seem to "travel" very well from potter to potter.

A little more explanation of flocculated vs. deflocculated suspensions is needed to help us decide which we want and what to change to get what we want. Well flocculated suspensions are characterized by 1) slow settling of the glaze materials in the container and 2) rapid absorption of water into the bisque surface which results in a thicker glaze layer and more rapid "drying" of the glaze on the pot so it can be handled more quickly. This 2nd characteristic is not very obvious and some would even say it is counter-intuitive; however it is well addressed in easy-to-understand terms in a series of *Clay Times* articles (Pinnell, March/April and May/June 1998). Glaze suspensions can also be over-flocculated. When this happens the suspension will become very thick and the tendency is to add more water to thin it down. If the water level is too high, then the bisque cannot absorb enough and glaze coating will be too thin and/or dry slowly. Another problem caused by over-flocculated, thinned glaze slurries is that they have a tendency to crawl. The excess water will result in high glaze shrinkage as the glaze dries.

Deflocculated suspensions are characterized by 1) more rapid settling, 2) hard-panning of glaze ingredients on the bottom of the container and 3) slower absorption of water into the bisque pot resulting in a thinner layer of glaze and slower "drying" of the glaze on the pot. Unfortunately, as noted in the paragraph above, this third characteristic can also be seen in an over-flocculated glaze making problem analysis more difficult.

Normally we want a well flocculated (but not over-flocculated) suspension when applying glazes by dipping or spraying; however we may want it less well flocculated or bordering on deflocculated when applying by brush. This gives more time for the glaze suspension to flow and smooth out before it dries. Changing the balance between flocculation and deflocculation is straightforward but must be done with care because small changes in composition can have a large effect.

Perhaps the first thing to try if you need a better flocculated glaze is 1) addition of 1-2% bentonite or 2) replacement of any EPK with ball clay. Always try bentonite and/or ball clay before any of the other techniques described below; they are insoluble materials and will cause less trouble. If you replace EPK with ball clay be sure to do it by holding the Seger molecular formula constant and calculating the correct adjustments—this is not a one-to-one substitution. If you need additional flocculation, the most

> **Other materials that are sometimes used to help a glaze stay in suspension are CMC or gum arabic. Some people even put sugar or corn syrup in their glaze mix; however this can result in an extremely smelly glaze slurry in a few days when the bacteria population explodes. The authors don't recommend any of these materials over those covered in the body of the text.**

common and readily available flocculent is Epsom salts (magnesium sulfate). A half-gallon carton of Epsom salts can be purchased at almost any pharmacy in North America and probably elsewhere in the world as well. One carton will last many years. Calcium chloride or muriatic (hydrochloric) acid are also available compounds which can be used as a flocculent. A splash of vinegar will provide immediate, but temporary flocculation. To use Epsom salts try adding about 1/2 gram dissolved in a small amount of warm water per 1000 grams of dry glaze ingredients. Thoroughly mix for a few minutes, test and repeat if necessary.

If you need better brushability, try adding a small amount of glycerine (available at drug stores in North America). If you decide to deflocculate your glaze slurry for better brushing performance try adding small amounts of Darvan 7, sodium carbonate (soda ash) or sodium silicate. While soda ash and sodium silicate are the more traditional deflocculants, many potters are switching to Darvan 7 because its effect is more gradual and easily controlled.

The glaze recipes given in Chapter 6 should not need much, if any, adjustment by these techniques. All of our recipes have enough clay in them to give reasonably stable suspensions. While all glaze suspensions should be well mixed and rescreened if they have been sitting more than a few hours, our recipes should yield glazes that stay suspended over the course of a couple hours glazing session with only an occasional quick stir.

Bisque Preparation

Bisque Firing

You can start endless debates about the best temperature for bisque firing. Of course some potters don't bisque at all, preferring to glaze leather hard or bone dry greenware. Other potters prefer to bisque as low as Cone 010-08 believing that the ware is strong enough to handle and they are saving money. Still others bisque in the 06-04 range. We come down strongly on the side of bisque firing to cone 04. Our experience has been that there are fewer problems in the glaze firing such as pinholes and quartz dunting with the higher temperature bisque. In addition, since the bisque ware is less absorbent at cone 04 you can work with less water in your glaze slurry. This results in more stable glaze suspensions and more uniform glaze application with less stirring. The minor savings in cost by bisque firing lower will not justify many ruined pots. Bisque firing at cone 04 is even more important as the size of your work increases. While lower bisque temperature may work well on small pots, the problems mentioned above are much more likely to occur on large pots.

> If you have over-flocculated or over-deflocculated it is often better to correct by adding fresh glaze rather than adding more chemicals to a glaze slurry.

Basics of Glazing and Firing

Cleaning

All bisqueware is dusty to a certain degree. Take time to wipe it inside and out with a barely damp sponge or cloth prior to glazing. Dust interferes with glaze adhesion and can result in crawling. While this is not a problem with many glazes it always seems to occur at the worst possible time. Be safe rather than sorry. Make sure that the sponge or cloth is barely damp; you do not want a wet pot as you get ready to apply glaze.

Glaze Resists

It is a matter of personal preference whether or not to wax the foot of a pot ready to be glazed vs. wiping glaze off afterward with a damp sponge or towel. We will describe several techniques that work; choose what works best for you.

Using melted paraffin wax is a common way of protecting the foot of a pot. The downside is that the hot wax is often smelly and, of course, there is the danger of setting it on fire if it is accidentally over-heated. If you use melted wax, always do it in a well ventilated area as the fumes can be toxic. We successfully and safely use this technique by melting it in a pan on a temperature-controlled hot plate or in a temperature controlled electric skillet. Set the temperature controller to about 120°C (about 250°F).

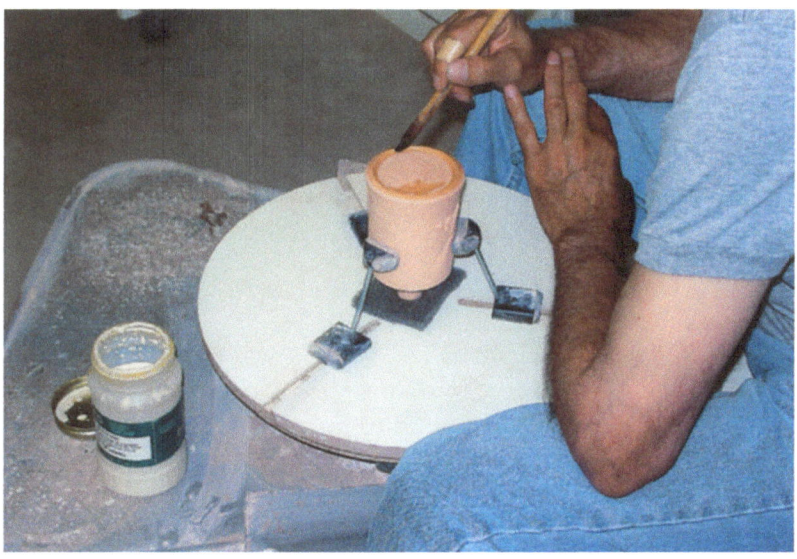

Figure 2-4. Ron nearly always applies wax on the wheel using a Giffen Grip® to help stabilize a small-necked pot.

and do not leave the room while the heat is turned on. If the wax starts to smoke or fume turn the heat down. The wax is at the right temperature if it is not smoking or fuming and it quickly and smoothly coats the bisqueware surface. Hot wax has resulted in many bad burns – make sure children and pets cannot get near it!

Wax dispersions, available from pottery supply houses, can also be used. They can be brushed on and there is no problem with fuming during application nor is there any danger from fire. Rotating the pot on your wheel allows easy and accurate application of wax dispersions. Selection of the right brush is also important to smooth, uniform application. Test several brushes until you find one that works well for you. Wax dispersions sometimes take several hours to dry thoroughly so this method requires planning ahead. Cleaning your brush out with soap and warm water at the end of the session will normally allow it to be used again.

Using a very damp terry cloth towel can be an effective way to remove glaze from the bottom of a pot. Lay the wet towel on a flat surface. After dipping the pot in glaze let it dry just enough to be able to handle it without damaging the glaze surface, then immediately place the pot on the towel and rotate it until the bottom is scrubbed clean. It may be necessary to use a damp sponge to remove the last traces of glaze. Don't do this with dry glaze as it generates too much dust.

Applying Glazes

Application of glazes is where individual creativity should come to bear so that the glaze enhances the beauty of your pot. While any number of books have thorough discussions of the various techniques for applying glazes there are some specific points we would like to make.

Figure 2-5. A glaze we call Variegated Blue (See Chapter 6 for the recipe) applied quite thinly to a tan stoneware pot.

Figure 2-6. Variegated Blue applied at normal thickness to porcelain.

First, it is critical that you get to know your glazes very well. It is foolish to test a glaze one time on one type of clay and decide it is something you like or don't like. Glazes look very different on various clay bodies. Thickness and evenness of application can cause glazes to be dramatically different in appearance. See Figures 2-5 and 2-6 for some examples of exactly the same glaze applied on different clays and at different thickness. It is hard to believe this is the same glaze and provides yet another reason why glazes often don't travel well between potters. This illustrates why it is a good idea to focus on only one or two glazes that you really like and learn how to use them well. You **must** know your glazes well if you are to get the best from them.

Second, it is usually helpful to know what glaze you are going to put on a pot as you make the piece. By doing this you can tailor the finishing touches on the pot to take advantage of the characteristics of the glaze. For example, if the glaze breaks nicely over texture and edges you may want to accentuate your edges or have sharp changes in direction rather than rounded ones. Or you might want to do some slip trailing or texturing with stamps or found objects.

Being able to coat the pot uniformly with glaze is usually desirable. Dipping is probably the easiest way to achieve this although if the pot has no irregular features, like a handle or a spout, spraying can be done very

Good sources of glaze application information are *Pottery Glazes* by David Green, *Ceramics: Mastering the Craft* by Richard Zakin and *The Ceramic Spectrum* by Robin Hopper. See the Bibliography for more complete information.

Whatever your glaze application technique, try to get a heavier coating of glaze toward the top tapering to a thinner layer at the bottom. For example, when dipping turn the pot upside down as quickly as possible after removing it from the glaze slurry.

uniformly too. Pouring is next best in achieving uniformity and brushing is usually the most difficult.

Firing

This is not a book on firing kilns, but there are several aspects of firing which directly affect the quality and the durability of the glazes on your pots.

Loading

The most important consideration in loading a kiln is to load it so you get uniform heat throughout the kiln. Most importantly don't stack too tightly. Leave at least one quarter inch between each pot and one half inch between the top of the tallest pot and the shelf directly above it. If you are firing with an electric kiln make sure you have at least one coil between every pair of shelves and put taller pots on the bottom shelf so you have two rows of elements available for heating the bottom of the kiln. If you are firing with gas it will take many firings before you learn how to stack and fire to get uniform heat, but the time spent will be well worth it.

Our next recommendation on loading is to put a cone pack of large cones on every shelf. At least occasionally, put a cone in the middle and one at the edge of one of your shelves. If they read differently, center to outside, you are firing too fast. Make sure at least two cone packs are visible from peep holes, but put cones on every shelf even if one of your shelves is between two peep holes. If you feel a cone pack on every shelf is not affordable at least use a single cone (the cone to which you are firing) on each shelf and a cone pack in front of the middle or top peephole. This is extremely important when you are trying to make any kiln fire evenly. Computer controlled kilns are great and Kiln Sitters® can be useful; however the only way to be certain about the temperature conditions your pots and glazes see is to have cones throughout the kiln. Figure 2-7 shows the level of uniformity that can readily be achieved if you pay attention to this aspect of your firing.

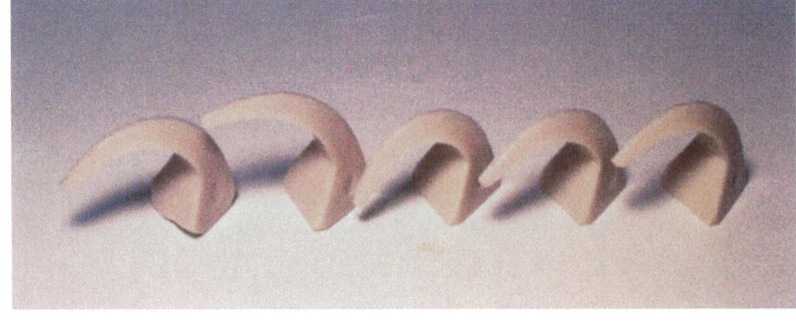

Figure 2-7. Five cones placed throughout the kiln during a glaze firing. In this particular firing 3 shelves were used and the kiln has a 3-zone computer controller.

Rate of Firing and Cooling

Controlling the rate of temperature rise and fall is as important for proper development of glazes as is firing to the correct temperature or cone. Unfortunately this is not widely understood and is, in fact, hindered by the terribly underinsulated electric kilns made by most kiln manufacturers. Going slowly the final 50-150°C (90-270°F) on top temperature is not too much of a problem, as many kilns are not capable of increasing temperature very rapidly when the kiln gets above 1000°C (1832°F). A slow approach to peak temperature is important, however, for several reasons. First you want uniform temperature throughout the kiln. Heat travels in an electric kiln by a combination of radiation, conduction, natural convection and forced convection; however radiation and conduction are far more important heat transfer mechanisms in an electric kiln than they are in a gas kiln where forced convection dominates. Radiation and conduction are slower processes and take time. Secondly, time is needed for glazes to chemically react and bond with the clay surface. This occurs primarily at or near the peak temperature.

Just as important is the cooling cycle. Turning a kiln off when it reaches temperature can be a mistake, as the temperature will drop very quickly. While this can be satisfactory for glossy glazes, it can be a disaster for properly formulated mattes and semimatte or satin glazes. These need to be cooled slowly to allow time for the crystals, which give the matte appearance, to form. By slowly, we recommend no faster than 80-100°C (about 150°F) per hour from about 1025 down to 800°C (1900 down to 1500°F). Going faster than this can easily cause a nice matte glaze to be semiglossy or even glossy. It is astonishing the difference cooling rate makes! An example of the computer-programmed cycle the authors use for glaze firing their electric kilns is given in Appendix E.

Summary

Glazing and firing are critical parts of making beautiful pottery that can be reliably reproduced. Too often they are regarded as undesirable tasks to be completed as quickly as possible so we can get back to more "important" creative work. However, the best potters realize that glazing and firing are important parts of the whole creative process. We believe most of us would benefit from focusing on only one or two glazes and learn to apply and fire them with great skill versus having a dozen glazes which we apply and fire with abandon. Taking the time to learn this aspect of pottery well will be worth it.

"As clothes are to the human body so are glazes to pots. Both serve practical ends, both should enhance inherent beauty of form. The covering of clay shapes with glazes, or glasses (for a glaze consists of, or resembles, a glass), makes them smoother to the touch, cleaner and more varied in colour and texture, and, in the case of pottery fired at low temperature, more impervious to fluids."

Bernard Leach, A Potter's Book

3
TESTING GLAZES FOR STABILITY AND FIT

It is easy to forget the relatively hard use that some glazes see during their lifetime on a functional piece of pottery. While giving care instructions to a person who purchases one of our pots can be a help in reducing exposure to harsh conditions, the fact of the matter is those instructions may soon be forgotten by most people. They will expect a hand made ceramic vessel to behave at least as well as its commercial counterpart. Whether we like it or not our pots will be put directly from the freezer into a warm or hot oven. They will have boiling water poured into them. They will be put in the dishwasher. They will be exposed to the acids in foods such as vinegar, lemon juice, tomato sauce, carbonated beverages and others. In today's world it is almost certain that our pottery will be used in microwave ovens whether or not we recommend it. It is not even hard to imagine someone using a bud vase as a sake decanter and heating it in a microwave oven. Once the pot leaves our hands we have no control over it and it may be used in unexpected ways. To the extent possible we should try to make a finished product which will withstand as many conditions as possible. The one use or exposure condition we will ignore is direct placement on stovetops. So-called "flameware" is very difficult to make and it is our opinion that, in today's litigious environment, a studio potter is foolish to try to produce it.

We divide the types of exposure a glaze/clay combination must withstand into several categories and discuss each of them separately. These are: 1) resistance to acids commonly found in foods, 2) resistance to alkalis such as dishwasher detergent, 3) resistance to thermal shock, 4) resistance to knife-marking (abrasion of the knife or other eating utensil which results in metallic marks being left on the pot), 5) resistance to scratching and wear (abrasion of the glaze), 6) resistance to chipping and 7) suitability for use in a microwave oven.

In the following paragraphs we will examine both in-studio and, in some cases, professional laboratory testing of glazes for the seven categories of exposure described above. In a subsequent chapter we will present ways of making glazes more resistant or more suitable for use in each of these situations.

Testing for Resistance to Acids

Most foods are acidic. A list developed by the U.S. Food and Drug Administration of the pH (the universal measurement of the degree of acidity) of various foods shows foods ranging in pH from 1.8 to 9.5 with more than 95% of them being on the acidic end of the scale (anything below 7.0 is acidic). Some of the most extreme situations that a ceramic glaze will see are things such as 1) a tomato-based dish baked in an oven for several hours, 2) a slice of lemon squeezed and set aside on a plate or saucer, 3) fruit juice stored in a pitcher or 4) a vinegar and oil salad dressing used in a salad bowl or stored in a cruet set. Unfortunately, of the thousands of glaze recipes circulating among potters, there are some very unstable glazes at all cones. Sometimes these recipes travel by word of mouth and sometimes they are published in well-regarded books. They are undoubtedly being used by some potters on functional work and, while we have no hard data, our experience indicates more than half of the functional glazes in use today would not pass the tests we are recommending in this book. Many of these glazes are very attractive and look very similar to glazes that are stable: You cannot tell if a glaze will be resistant to acids just by looking at it. The glazes illustrated in Chapter 1, Figures 1-1 through 1-3 illustrate this point well. These were very attractive glazes, which failed almost immediately on exposure to lemon juice. We don't believe any potters would want these glazes on their functional work in spite of their visual attractiveness. There are two ways we recommend testing glazes to assure good resistance to acids: 1) an in-studio test involving soaking the glaze in vinegar and 2) professional leach testing.

We will describe and examine both types of testing, but first, special mention needs to be made of one material in particular: copper. Use of copper in glazes for use on functional pottery is controversial in some people's minds. Copper can be safely used in lead-free functional glazes; however, it is one of the most difficult materials to work with when it comes to acid stability. Part of the reason that copper is controversial is because it is well documented in the literature (Taylor and Bull, page 180 among many other references) that the presence of copper destabilizes a lead-based glaze causing more lead to leach out of the glaze when it is exposed to acidic conditions. It is also true that copper is one of the most difficult materials to keep in a glaze—leaded or lead free. You have to pay attention to what you are doing to make a stable copper-colored glaze, but stable glazes can be made that contain up to 5% copper carbonate. Copper is one of our favorite materials to use in testing a new base glaze. If a glaze will hold 5% copper carbonate with minimal leaching of copper, it is very likely to be stable with normal levels of other colorants. Note that our standard challenge test is to add 5% copper carbonate <u>and</u> 5-6% rutile—we'll explain the rutile later. More will be said on the use of copper in Chapter 4.

> A word about copper carbonate: We usually test our glazes with 5% copper carbonate and 5-6% rutile and use that leaching level as a reference point as we have on this page. The copper carbonate we use, and which is readily available to potters, is $Cu(OH)_2 \cdot CuCO_3$. It is also a mineral called malachite. Its molecular weight is 221.11 or 110.56 per unit of copper. Copper is also available to potters as black (cupric) copper oxide (CuO; M.W.= 79.54) and red (cuprous) copper oxide (Cu_2O; M.W. = 143.08). If you use one of these other forms of copper the equivalent amounts would be:
> 5% copper carbonate =
> 3.6% black copper oxide =
> 3.24% red copper oxide.

In-Studio Testing

Vinegar is one of the more acidic materials a glaze will encounter making it an ideal substance for in-studio testing. It is inexpensive and readily available at a standard 5% acetic acid concentration. Always start by thoroughly cleaning your test sample with soap and water. It is important to make sure no greasy fingerprints interfere with the test. We have found that soaking part of a glaze test coupon in vinegar for a period of 3 days at normal room temperature provides a good screening test of a glaze's resistance to acid. A simple way to do this is shown in Figure 3-1 where an extruded angular test tile has been set on the edge of a glass containing vinegar so that about half of the glazed surface is exposed to the vinegar.

Figure 3-1. The vinegar test is easily done by inserting half of a glazed test coupon in vinegar for 3 days. The samples on the left illustrate various degrees of failure while the ones on the right passed.

After 3 days the sample is removed, carefully washed and dried. It is important here, not only to dry the sample with a towel, but also to let it sit for a few minutes so any residual water molecules evaporate. Then examine the sample both with your naked eye and with low power magnification (10X). Magnifying glasses of this power are readily available at coin and stamp dealers or hobby shops. If you see any change in color or surface sheen in the exposed surface this glaze is probably quite unstable and not suitable for functional pottery. The only exception to this we have experienced is an extremely glossy glaze that had just the slightest change in surface sheen. In later quantitative testing (described below) it turned out to be quite stable. All things considered then, this screening test is quite useful for initial testing of a glaze obtained from a book or another potter as well as for one you have formulated yourself. **It will not tell you with certainty that a glaze is stable,** but it can keep you from spending more time and effort on a glaze that is unstable. Quantitative testing is the only way to determine how resistant a glaze is to acids.

Quantitative Testing by a Professional Testing Laboratory

A better and more quantitative way to determine the stability to acids of a glaze is to have it leach-tested by a professional laboratory. The test we use is the same used for testing for lead and/or cadmium in glazes. It involves leaching the glaze for 24 hours with 4% acetic acid solution at room temperature and then accurately measuring materials in the leachate via atomic absorption spectrophotometry. Testing the leachate for all oxides that might be in the glaze can be quite expensive so some judicious choices must be made regarding what to test for. Testing for the basic components in a glaze such as silica and alumina is seldom worthwhile. We tend to focus on the colorants that are in the glaze and, in particular, those where there might be some toxicity concern if they leached in large amounts. For example, we rarely test for iron, but will usually test for copper, cobalt, nickel, manganese and chromium if they are used in a particular glaze. With respect to fluxes we would always test for barium if we used it (which we do not do on functional pottery). Occasionally we test for materials like zinc or boron if they are present in large quantities. Normally, though, testing for one or two things will give you a good idea of overall glaze stability to acids.

Results from professional laboratory leach testing in North America will be reported in milligrams per liter (mg/l) or parts per million (ppm). These are numerically the same numbers with mg/l now the more standard way of reporting small concentrations of materials. In Europe, and perhaps other parts of the world, the standard way of reporting leach testing for ceramic ware is more likely to be milligrams per square decimeter. The difference is that the European method takes into account the relative surface area of the vessel being tested—an important consideration. In our work (and our recommendation to you) we use standard size containers so that our results can readily be converted from the North American standard of mg/l to the European standard of mg/dm^2. The containers we use are thrown from about 1 lb (454 g) of clay and have wet dimensions of 4 inches (10+ cm) in diameter by 3 inches (7.5+ cm) high. After firing the dimensions are such that about 150 square centimeters (1.5 square decimeters) of surface area are exposed to the acid.

Nearly any laboratory that tests water quality or does environmental testing will have the equipment necessary to do this kind of testing. However, because there is a relatively low demand for testing the acid resistance of ceramic glazes, few laboratories have developed the procedures to do so. The labs we know of who do this type of testing in North America at a reasonable cost are listed in Appendix D.

Interpretation of Results

Interpreting results of quantitative leach test results requires some judgment and background knowledge. In the United States there are no standards of "acceptable" or "unacceptable" levels of leaching except for lead and cadmium. For those materials, the U.S. Food and Drug Administration has specified the maximum permissible levels for leaching. Since we don't work with lead and cadmium and do not recommend them for use on functional pottery we need other reference points. Most other areas in the world have similar standards; although barium is regulated in some countries and manganese in others. There may be a few other places where additional materials are regulated—a functional potter must always be familiar with the regulations in her own country or countries where her pottery is sold.

One set of reference points we find useful are the primary, and to a lesser extent, the secondary water standards for drinking water. Primary U.S. water standards of interest to potters are shown in Table 3-1; secondary standards can be found in Appendix H. It could certainly be said that, if an aggressive test like leaching for 24 hours with 4% acetic acid results in a lower concentration of metal in the acid leachate than would be allowed in drinking water, there would certainly be no safety or health concern. We are not in any way recommending that primary drinking water standards be used as a standard against which to judge the leaching performance of glazes. There are no data to support adoption of such a standard and, indeed, the FDA standards for lead and cadmium extracted from ceramic glazes are from 7 to 200 times higher than the standards for lead and cadmium in drinking water depending on the type of ceramic vessel being tested. Primary drinking water standards, where they exist for materials of interest to potters, do represent a useful reference point at the very conservative end of the spectrum. Many glazes can be made which will meet drinking water standards and some potters may wish to adopt these numbers as their own personal goals.

Contaminant	MCL* in mg/l
Barium	2.0
Cadmium	0.005
Chromium	0.1
Copper	1.3
Lead	0.015
Nickel	0.1

*MCL is the maximum contaminant level permissible.

Table 3-1. Primary water standards for materials of interest to potters

Use of water standards has some serious shortcomings, however. First, as noted above, they are very stringent, particularly when compared to the standards for use of lead and cadmium in ceramic ware. Therefore their use might preclude using some materials and/or glaze formulations for no sound reason. Equally important is that there are no water standards for some materials of interest to potters. Even ignoring those materials about which there is essentially no toxicity concern such as calcium, sodium, potassium and magnesium, entirely missing from the water standards are commonly used materials like cobalt and lithium. Of course some of the less commonly used materials like vanadium are also not covered by a water standard.

Perhaps a more useful set of reference points could be assembled by looking at all of the data we have compiled for the glazes we and others have tested and look at the range of results obtained. At our current stage of knowledge this data set will also have some holes in it because, although we have done more testing than anyone else (as measured from the publicly

Material	Total Range of Data, mg/l	The Stable End of the Spectrum, mg/l
Chromium	Insufficient Data*	
Cobalt	0.0-3.2	<0.2
Copper	0.1-60	<6.0
Manganese	0.0-0.8	<0.2
Nickel	Insufficient Data*	

In the testing of the glazes in this book we have not measured numbers higher than the detectable limit of 0.02 mg/l; however we have used only low levels of these colorants. Glazes tested by others, where we are aware of the results, have rarely used these colorants. We have too few data points to make any definitive statement at this time.

Table 3-2. The range of leaching data obtained for glazes studied

available literature), we recognize our data set is far from comprehensive. We pledged in the introduction to this book that we would only offer glaze recipes that are far toward the stable end of the spectrum. Table 3-2 shows what our data indicates to be levels of leachates for the materials we have measured as of this writing and within that data set the levels that we consider to be well into stable end of the spectrum.

Ultimately each potter must set his own goals in this area. There is simply not enough information available at this point in time to objectively set goals. Nor is better information likely to become available any time soon. Determining objective standards based on health or aesthetic considerations (e.g. copper is known to make food taste bitter at about 5-10 mg/l) would require a vast amount of research and, at this time, we are not aware that such research is underway.

Testing for Resistance to Alkalis

Resistance to alkaline materials is an entirely different matter than resistance to acids; however, many glazes resistant to one are resistant to the other for different reasons. We will learn in the next chapter that silica and alumina levels are important to acid resistance. It is reported (Taylor and Bull, pages 170-173) that zinc oxide, zirconia and alumina all improve alkaline resistance. Eppler and Eppler (pages 261-263) confirm the importance of these three materials to alkaline resistance and give more specific information on useful ranges.

Exposure of glazes to alkaline materials occurs primarily in the dishwasher. There are a few alkaline foods; however, they are a tiny minority. Simulating the dishwasher environment, then, is the essential part of testing our glazes for alkaline resistance. The simplest test is simply to put a sample cup in a dishwasher and leave it there. If the glaze is very unstable it will begin to show evidence of fading within 30 cycles or so; however simulating an acceptable life of a glaze via exposure in a dishwasher requires a longer test than is reasonable. Therefore an accelerated test is needed.

Over the years a number of such tests have been proposed and used to test alkali resistance. One test, used to some extent by the dinnerware industry, is to submerge a test sample in a 5% sodium carbonate (potters usually call this soda ash) solution and hold it at 98°C for 6 hours. Sodium carbonate or soda ash is a major component of many dishwasher detergents so exposing a glaze to this material does provide a good approximation of the dishwasher chemical environment. A visual comparison is then made with an untested sample. The test is said to simulate about 250 dishwasher cycles. Another method for testing porcelain enamels which is sanctioned by the American Society for Testing and Materials (ASTM), and published by them as ASTM Standard Test Method C614-74, is to expose carefully weighed samples to a 5% solution of tetrasodium pyrophosphate. The exposure is for 6 hours at a temperature of 96°C. Samples are then measured for weight loss.

Since few potters have access to a temperature controlled bath or a high precision balance needed to carry out these procedures exactly as specified, we devised a test that can be performed in a studio or home situation. The test we propose is as follows:

Make a 5% soda ash solution (e.g. 50 grams of soda ash in 1 liter of water). Put this solution in a stainless steel pan (no aluminum please) and bring it to a boil on your stove. Reduce the heat so the liquid will just continue to simmer gently. Place your samples in the pan, cover and continue simmering for six hours. Covering the pan will, of course, minimize

> Normal safety precautions must be taken when performing this test. Sodium carbonate solution is mildly caustic or alkaline and, as such, can severely damage eyes and other sensitive tissue. Care must be taken to prevent such exposure by wearing safety goggles and gloves when handling this solution.

evaporation. The pan should be checked periodically and additional water added if necessary to keep the liquid level constant. On completion, cool, rinse and compare the color and surface gloss of the samples with untested control samples. The goal is no visible change. A moderately stable glaze may have a very slight gloss change, but no color change. Glazes that visibly fade should be considered to be of highly questionable stability for multiple dishwashings over a period of years.

At least one color variant of all of the base glazes shown in Chapter 6 and all of the specialty glazes have been tested by this procedure. Most passed with no visible change; where there was a change it is noted and described. A glaze obtained from the published literature that was known by the authors to be unstable to acid leaching was also tested by this procedure. A significant fading and etching of the glaze surface occurred. While this would appear to be an effective screening test, we have not evaluated it to the point we can say it equates to some specific number of dishwashing cycles. It is, however, a very close approximation of tests used by industry for similar materials and we feel very confident that a glaze that is durable in this test will have a long life in home dishwashing.

Another accelerated test has been devised by the ASTM. It is specifically for measuring the removal of overglaze patterns from tableware by dishwater detergents. It involves holding samples in solutions of the detergents to be tested at elevated temperatures for 2-hour periods. Samples are then evaluated by vigorously rubbing the decoration with muslin cloth and looking for pigment removed. Details of this procedure can be found in ASTM Standard Test Method D3565.

Testing for Resistance to Thermal Shock (Clay/Glaze Fit)

Achieving a good fit of clay and glaze will be covered in detail in a later chapter. Here we will define what we mean by clay/glaze fit and describe how to test for it. When clay and its attached glaze are heated or cooled they always change very slightly in size albeit at different rates. This is no different than roads that expand, and sometimes buckle, in hot weather or shrink and leave large gaps between sections of pavement in cold weather. The difference we must deal with is that the clay and glaze are tightly bonded together and, if they don't expand or contract at approximately the same rate, serious defects can occur. The first is called crazing and occurs when the glaze contracts on cooling significantly more than the clay. The result can be a network of hairline cracks in the glaze surface. The reverse phenomena happens when the glaze contracts significantly less on cooling than the clay. In extreme cases this results in shivering (razor sharp slivers coming off the pot) and/or dunting (cracking during cooling or use). Neither crazing nor shivering/dunting is desirable in functional pottery; although a case could be made that shivering/dunting is the more dangerous phenomenon. It

> Perhaps a simpler way to describe crazing and shivering is to say that on cooling, crazing results when the glaze ends up smaller than the clay, i.e. it contracts more than the clay. Shivering results when the glaze ends up bigger than the clay, i.e. it contracts less.

often goes unnoticed until the pot is in your customer's hands. Shivering is probably less common; although it occurs more often than it should. Shivering usually only occurs when a very low expansion flux like Li_2O or MgO is in a glaze in a significant amount, when substantial cristobalite has been formed by having excess silica in the clay body or by overfiring. Our focus in the following paragraphs will be on crazing; however the same tests will also cause shivering or dunting to occur if that is likely.

Many potters get the first indication of crazing when they remove their pots from the kiln. Do you ever hear those little "pings" coming from your pottery as it sits on the shelf in the first hours, or even days, after it is removed from the kiln? That is crazing; the glaze is actually cracking apart and forming that network of lines mentioned above. Testing more formally for craze resistance can be done in one of two ways. Both involve thermally shocking some of your pots.

The first method is one commonly used by studio potters because it is quick and easy. Place test pots in a freezer and leave them there for several hours. Boil some water in a teakettle or other pan that will allow easy pouring. Quickly remove a pot from the freezer and place it in a sink. Immediately fill it with boiling water. This is done in a sink to minimize chances of splashing yourself with boiling water; however it obviously still must be done very carefully. After a few minutes pour the water out and dry the pot. Carefully examine it for shivering or crazing. A handheld magnifier is very useful for seeing these defects. If you are not accustomed to looking for crazing it might help to 1) apply ink to the surface of the pot with a felt tip marker, 2) remove the ink with a suitable solvent and 3) then examine the surface. Ink will normally remain in the craze lines, if they are present, and they will be easier to see. It is very difficult to see craze lines in a dark glaze. Hold the pot over boiling water and let steam condense on the surface; then look carefully for crazing. Repeat this freezing-to-boiling-water test 3 or more times. Even after testing it may take days or even weeks for crazing to develop in a marginal case. This is especially so with boron-containing glazes. Recheck your samples every week for several weeks to be sure they haven't crazed.

Another test is the one sanctioned by the ASTM (ASTM C 554-93). It involves heating test pots in an oven and immediately quenching the pots in pans of room temperature water. Clearly, great care must also be exercised here to avoid burning yourself with the hot pots. The procedure requires starting the test at 121°C (250°F) and progressing to higher temperatures. The ASTM procedure states that pots that pass 3 cycles at 149°C (300°F) "can be expected to resist crazing under all normal conditions of service." This test is more rigorous than the one above because the thermal shock is somewhat greater and it is more extended. For complete details on this test, see the referenced ASTM procedure.

Testing for Resistance to Knife Marking

We have all seen knife marked, or more properly, metal marked pottery. These marks are simply caused by a ceramic surface abrading metal from a utensil and that metal is deposited on the glaze surface. This is much more of a problem with matte glazes than it is with glossy glazes; although glossy or semi-gloss glazes do not seem immune. It is, however, one of the primary reasons we do not use dry matte or matte glazes on functional surfaces. We don't recommend anything more matte than a semimatte or satin for food surfaces. Mattes and dry mattes can certainly be used on functional pottery, but we believe they are best reserved for the outside surfaces of vases, mugs and the like.

The best test for knife marking is simply to use your pottery yourself. It is always easier to see on white or light colored glazes and you will know after a few months whether or not this is a problem for a particular glaze. This test takes time and an accelerated version would be useful. Perhaps the easiest test is to take any coin, knife or metal tool (a coin or the handle end of a pair of pliers are the testing implements of choice for the authors). Firmly drag that metal across the glazed surface to be tested. After a few tries with both a glossy and a matte glaze you will learn how much pressure to use to leave metal marks. Repeat several times and examine the surface carefully. The marks you see (if any) are tiny particles of the metal which have been abraded by the ceramic surface. They will lodge in microscopic crevices of the glaze and can be easy or difficult to remove. If you can remove them by rubbing with your thumb they are probably at a satisfactory level. The best situation is, of course, not to have made any visible marks. Sometimes the marks will not come off even after vigorous scrubbing with a scouring powder. If they are this difficult to remove the glaze should not be used on surfaces subject to metal contact such as plates, insides of bowls and cups, etc. It is also important to point out that a glaze that is attacked by acids or bases will metal mark more badly over time. The etching from the acids/bases will leave a rougher surface that will abrade metal more easily and be more difficult to clean.

Testing for Wear and Scratch Resistance

There is no simple in-studio test that we have been able to find or devise for testing wear and scratching of a glazed surface. One we have tried that frankly hasn't shown us much is to test the hardness of the glaze using simple "scratch testers". These are a set of pen-like instruments tipped with materials of different hardness. They typically range from Mohs' scale hardness of 5.5-9.0. Most glazes can be scratched with a "7" pen (quartz), but not with a "6" pen (orthoclase feldspar). We have not found this to be differentiating enough to be useful.

Using your pottery yourself for an extended period of time is, of course, one way to test for wear and scratch resistance. It is very likely that if you are making "good enough glass" to have satisfactory resistance to acid leaching you will not have a problem with wear and scratching of your glaze surfaces.

Testing for Chipping Resistance

One of the primary causes of poor chip resistance is poor adhesion between clay and glaze. The tests for clay/glaze fit described above will also reveal poor adhesion.

Testing for Suitability for Use in a Microwave Oven

Microwave ovens are everywhere these days and it is almost inevitable that a piece of functional pottery will be used in one. Overglazing with things like a metallic luster is almost certain to cause problems in a microwave and should be avoided on functional pottery. Other than that, there is really only one overriding factor that makes a pot suitable or not suitable for use in a microwave oven: Is the clay well vitrified? If it is well vitrified, there will likely not be a problem in a microwave; if it is not well vitrified it will, more than likely, overheat and perhaps cause scalding or burning of the person removing it from the microwave oven. It could even crack or explode.

The reason for the focus on vitrification here is straightforward. Microwave ovens are designed to heat water. While they will transfer energy in small amounts to other materials also, those materials are insignificant compared to the effect on water. Microwaves heat the water molecules in food and, thereby, the entire mass of food becomes warm or hot. If clay is not well vitrified it will absorb too much water during, for example, dishwashing, and that water will cause the pot to get hot during microwave heating. The total amount of water that can be absorbed by fired clays ranges from almost 0% for a well fired porcelain to 10-15% for normally fired earthenware. The exact amount in the clay at any point in time is dependent on its recent history. If it has just been through the dishwasher it will have more; if it has been sitting on the shelf for a long time during winter when the humidity is low it will have less. So the key question is how much water is too much. The answer seems to be in the range of 2-3%. This also happens to be the approximate moisture absorption level of well-vitrified stoneware . Earthenware, on the other hand, will almost always be a problem in a microwave unless it has been totally encased in an excellent glaze.

There is one other factor that should be considered in determining suitability for use in a microwave. There are some data that indicate high levels of metal in glazes can result in pots heating up in a microwave. We have not seen this ourselves, but it is something to consider.

Testing for performance in a microwave is really quite simple. It can be done by careful measurement of the water absorption of a test sample or fired pot. This is a number you should check for other reasons to make sure your clay is properly vitrified. It is a very simple test to do. Take an unglazed, but glaze fired test tile 1 or 2 inches wide by 3 to 5 inches long x 0.5 inch thick. The size is not critical although making it too thin can increase the error because of relatively more surface area for water evaporation. On the other hand, if it is too thick water may not penetrate all the way into the test sample. Immediately on opening the kiln, carefully weigh it and record the weight. Do not delay doing this or the result will be in error because of pickup of atmospheric moisture. Weigh the sample while it is still warm. Submerge the tile in a pan of water and gently boil it for at least two hours. Let the test sample cool to room temperature while it is still submerged. When the test tile is cool, quickly remove it from the pan, dry it carefully and promptly weigh it again. The fractional moisture absorption is calculated by [*boiled weight-original weight*] / [*original weight*]. To convert to percentage, multiply by 100. If you want a more rigorous and accurate determination of water absorption see ASTM C373-88—the procedure used by the whiteware industry which has been carefully validated.

Another technique to directly check suitability in a microwave oven is to take a mug and immerse it in a pan of water. Bring the water to a boil and let it simmer for a couple hours. This will assure that the mug has absorbed as much water as it will under the worst circumstances. Dry the mug and put it in the microwave oven empty. Also put another glass or mug full of water in the microwave at the same time. This step is essential and you may damage your microwave if you don't do it. Turn the microwave on high for 10 seconds at a time—**no more**. Stop the microwave, open the door and **carefully** touch the empty mug. If it is too hot to pick up with your bare hands it is not suitable for use in the microwave. Repeat these 10-second tests, carefully checking the temperature of the empty mug after each 10 seconds, until the water in the other vessel boils. If the empty mug can still be comfortably handled when the water is boiling, then the mug is microwave-safe. It is as simple as that. If, on the other hand, the empty mug has become too hot to handle during this test, the clay is not sufficiently vitrified and should not be used for functional pottery.

If you want to continue to use that clay you will need to fire it to a higher temperature and see if you get down to a satisfactory level of water absorption. The other option is, of course, to find a clay body that is properly vitrified at your firing temperature of choice. Good vitrification is important, of course, for more than performance in the microwave. For example, it is also required for a pot to hold water or a cruet set to hold oil without seeping even if the glaze has pinholes or is crazed. Glazing alone is often not enough to make a ceramic vessel water or oil tight.

Summary

All of this testing may seem like a lot of work; however for the most part it only needs to be done occasionally. You can do most of it in your studio with a minimum of expense other than time. Certainly it should be done when a new glaze and/or clay is developed or adopted into your studio. In addition we recommend you do at least some testing when other conditions change, such as a new lot of ingredients. If your clay supplier does not label each box with a lot number then you should test every box (or change clay suppliers—not providing lot numbers indicates a serious lack of interest in quality control). We would recommend buying glaze ingredients, at least the ones you use most, in 50 pound bags or multiples of 50 pound bags if you are a high production studio. Not only is the price far better, but you will be changing lots of materials far less often. By buying in 50 pound bags you will also eliminate errors that suppliers sometimes make when re-bagging materials.

Overall, this chapter has dealt with an often-ignored part of craftsmanship. Will our pottery, whether functional or decorative, be suitable for its intended purpose? While functional pottery provides the most demanding environment for a glaze, decorative work should not be made carelessly or without concern for the environment it will encounter. As has been noted earlier, tile murals may be cleaned with strong acids or bases. Outdoor sculptures will experience acid rain or bird droppings. Even a small indoor sculpture might find itself in a dishwasher on occasion. Good craftsmanship demands that we pay attention to how our work will be used as we design it.

"Art cannot exist without craftsmanship; but craftsmanship alone, even if you live forever will not make you into an artist. Yet it is quite correct to say that whereas the craftsman treats craftsmanship as an end in itself the artist treats it as a means to an end, because the two are so closely intergrown that it would fatally damage both to divide them into the categories of means and ends."

Michael Cardew, Pioneer Pottery

4

MAKING A STABLE GLAZE

Making stable glazes is still about two parts science and one part art, although we have made a lot of progress while developing the material for this book. The science is not well enough developed to assure the making of a stable glaze purely from knowledge of the chemistry or the composition of a glaze. We do know enough to dramatically improve your chances of making stable glazes by presenting a set of "rules" to follow. We will also present some "guidelines" which might further improve your chances of making stable glazes; however there is much less data to support these guidelines. Some words of explanation are in order.

In the early years of glaze research—from the time of Seger in the last half of the 19th century to about 1970—there were major efforts to understand the making of stable glazes. However, this work was done in an entirely different context. It was done with the objective of keeping lead in glazes. It was also done during a period of time when analytical instrumentation was primitive compared to that which is available today. Measurement of trace amounts of lead required a tedious laboratory analysis that was very time-consuming and not as accurate or precise as can be done in today's world. Hence the knowledge developed during that era, while developed by very talented people cannot be used directly with any confidence. We have had to develop our own rules and guidelines—sometimes confirming those of previous investigations and sometimes not.

The rules we present will result in stable glazes in most cases **provided** reasonable levels of colorants and opacifiers are used (actually that is also the last rule, but it is so important we want to mention it here as well). **Any** glaze can be made unstable by overloading it with either colorants or opacifiers. For example, we have yet to see a glaze that can hold 7-10% copper carbonate; 5% seems to be about the upper limit. In fact, we have done much of our test work at a glaze loading of 5% copper carbonate and 5-6% rutile. We have found that a glaze that will hold these amounts of additives and leach less than 6 mg/l of copper in the standard leaching test will nearly always hold reasonable levels of other colorants with minimal leaching.

The other thing that must be mentioned is that there may well be stable glazes outside of the rules we present; however we believe the chances of this occuring are small. We have only designated those things as rules for which we have substantial knowledge and data. Guidelines are a different matter. There certainly are good glazes outside the guidelines contained in this book. Again, it is a matter of odds. Your odds of success will be higher by staying within guidelines, but you may not be able to achieve the range of aesthetics you want. If one were to stay entirely within the rules AND the guidelines the range of aesthetics would probably be limited to glossy and semiglossy glazes. By staying within the rules, but going outside the guidelines, we can expand the range of aesthetics to include semimattes and even mattes.

Rule 1. Have Enough Silica

Silica is the backbone of a glaze. It is the primary glass former. Without sufficient silica you cannot make a stable glaze. We cannot stress that strongly enough. Figure 4-1 illustrates this point clearly.

The glazes represented by this graph were a carefully controlled set where only silica level was changed. All other parameters in the Seger unity formula were kept as constant as possible. The specific recipes are given in Appendix G. All samples were fired to Cone 6. While there is some scatter in this data, it is clear that leaching of copper is higher at low silica levels, comes down sharply with increasing silica and begins to level off at a silica level of about 3.0. Whether or not the leaching level starts to increase at silica levels above 4.0, as we have shown in Figure 4-1, is a

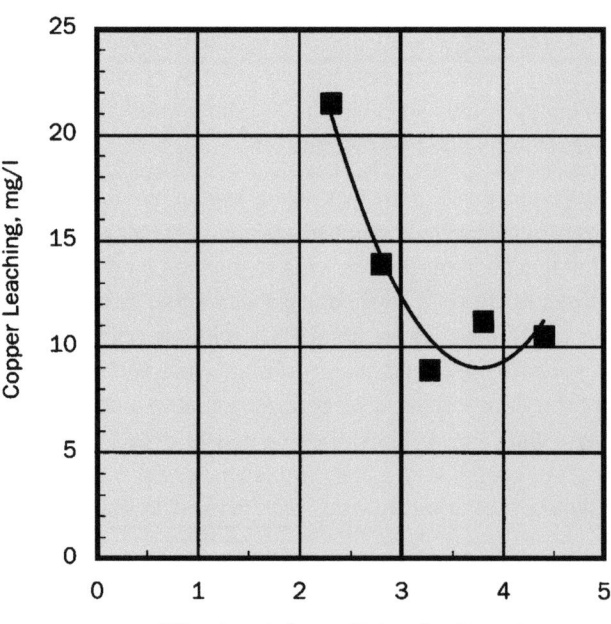

Figure 4-1. The effect of silica level on copper leaching for specific glaze compositions.

matter of conjecture. If it does start to increase it is probably because of Rule 3, which follows.

Rule 2. Have Enough Alumina

Potters long believed that you had to have a minimum level of alumina; however you can have too much if the balance of fluxes plus boron does not result in complete melting. Again, in a carefully controlled experiment where only the alumina level was varied, Figure 4-2 shows this effect.

Clearly, somewhere between 0.25 and 0.45 alumina is the place to be for optimum stability or minimum leaching of copper for this particular set of fluxes and levels of boron and silica. Whether this relationship holds true for all glaze compositions or only for the particular set of fluxes and silica level used for this experiment is unknown; however we believe it to be close to a generally useable relationship. It is quite likely that the increase in leaching at the higher alumina level is due to violation of Rule 3 rather than something inherently bad about high levels of alumina; although there are other mechanisms one could propose.

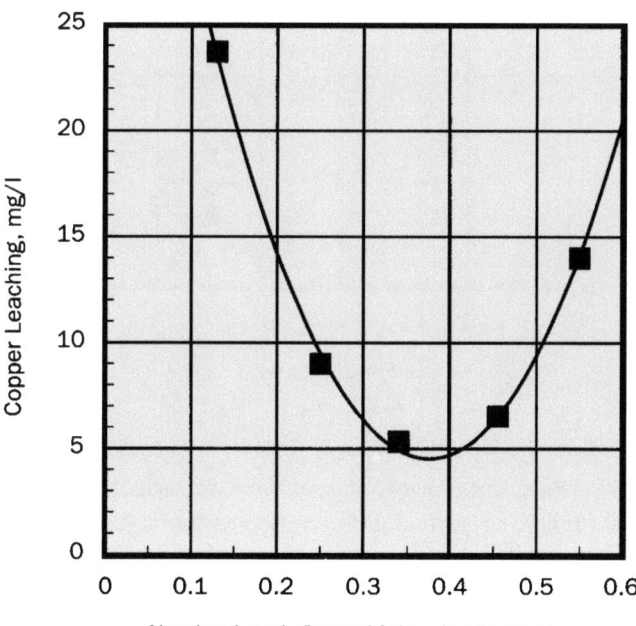

Figure 4-2. The effect of alumina level on the leaching of copper.

Rule 3. Thoroughly Melt the Glaze

An alternative way to state this rule might be that you must have an appropriate balance of fluxes combined with an appropriate level of boron to assure good melting given the silica and alumina levels you have chosen to use. This may seem to be an obvious rule—one that goes without saying—but it is not all that clear. Too many matte or semimatte glazes—perhaps most at Cone 6—being used today are matte because they have not been completely melted during firing. **Making matte glazes by incomplete melting is totally unsatisfactory in terms of stability.**

With glossy glazes, visual examination is a reasonable indicator of whether or not the glaze has been thoroughly melted. However with a high calcium semimatte glaze, for example, you cannot tell by visual observation. Figure 4-3 helps to make this point.

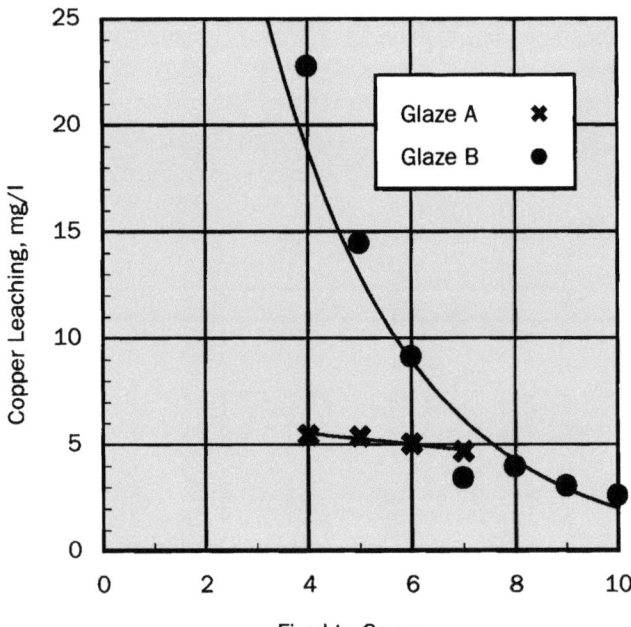

Figure 4-3. The effect of firing temperature.

It plots leaching data for two glazes (specific recipes in Appendix G) that were each fired to several different temperatures (cones). The glaze represented by the lower curve (Glaze A) was a glossy glaze that looked "mature" (it looked like it had been melted) at cone 4. There was very little difference in appearance of the samples up to and including cone 7. Indeed, the leaching data show that it was melted at cone 4. There is no significant difference in leaching between cone 4 and cone 7.

On the other hand, the glaze represented by the upper curve (Glaze B) was a high calcium semimatte. As you can see in Figure 4-4, there was relatively little difference in appearance to the naked eye in the final glaze from cone 4 through cone 7. Above cone 7 the glaze was slightly more glossy. Only careful microscopic examination by a skilled observer shows differences but even then it was not possible to detect the point where complete melting was achieved. However, the leaching performance dramatically improved up to about cone 7. Clearly, this glaze did not completely melt until about cone 7. It should be noted, however, that at cone 6 it is well enough melted to hold most colorants other than copper.

Figure 4-4. These test pots are glazed with Glaze B (Figure 4-3) and were fired to 4 different temperatures as shown by the cone packs. There is very little variation in appearance; however there is a big difference in leaching.

Since the visual differences between thoroughly melted and incompletely melted glazes are small, special care must be exercised to make sure you follow this rule. This is particularly so with semimatte and matte glazes. The best way to confirm that you have thoroughly melted a glaze is to leach test for extractable metals as described in Chapter 3.

Another point is that if you are following Rules 1, 2 and 4 and are still not getting the leaching performance you expected you should try firing at a higher temperature and see if performance improves. If it does, you were surely underfiring at the lower temperature.

Rule 4. Use Moderate Levels of Colorants and Opacifiers

As we pointed out in a preceeding paragraph, any glaze can be made unstable by overloading it with colorants and/or opacifiers. What then is the acceptable range of colorants to put in an otherwise stable glaze? Fortunately, the limits seem to be high enough that nearly all "normal" colorant levels are acceptable. In most cases the only colorant levels that will cause a glaze to become unstable are those that give so-called metallic effects.

In general, a level of colorants that is soluble in the base glaze will not cause stability problems if the base glaze itself is stable. We do not have completely accurate levels to recommend; however, from our limited testing and from what is known in the literature the levels shown in Table 4-1 are probably useable in an otherwise stable base glaze.

We must emphasize that when using any of these colorants, except iron oxide, we always leach-test before using them on a functional surface—particularly a surface that might be a food contact surface. Our views on how to select your own goals for maximum leaching levels are contained in Chapter 3.

Table 4-1. Approximate maximum levels of colorant that can be used and still have a stable glaze.

Colorant	Recommended Maximum level, % of the base glaze
Copper Carbonate	4.0
Copper Oxide	2.0-2.5
Chromium Oxide	3.0
Cobalt Carbonate	3.0
Cobalt Oxide	2.0
Iron Oxide	10.0-15.0
Manganese Dioxide	4.0
Nickel Oxide	3.0

We also would point out that combinations of colorants should be leach-tested. Just because a base glaze will hold, say, 4% copper carbonate and another variant of that glaze will hold 2% cobalt carbonate does not mean that a third variant with 4% copper **and** 2% cobalt will be stable.

A point that was made above but is worth repeating, is that any glaze can be made unstable by overburdening it with colorants. Almost any glaze that has a metallic look will leach significant amounts of colorant metals and cannot be recommended for functional surfaces. Words like "gun metal" or "metallic" in the name of the glaze are a clear warning flag.

Opacifiers are yet another consideration. While, for the most part, colorants are or should be glass-soluble in the base glaze, opacifiers work because they are not glass-soluble. The data we have developed on zircon (zirconium silicate) is shown in Figure 4-5. As usual, we developed these data by adding 5% copper carbonate to each glaze and testing for leaching of copper.

As you can see, zircon does not help glaze stability, at least in this instance. This graph flies in the face of the published literature that indicates zircon aids stability (Eppler and Eppler, page 261 and Taylor and Bull, page

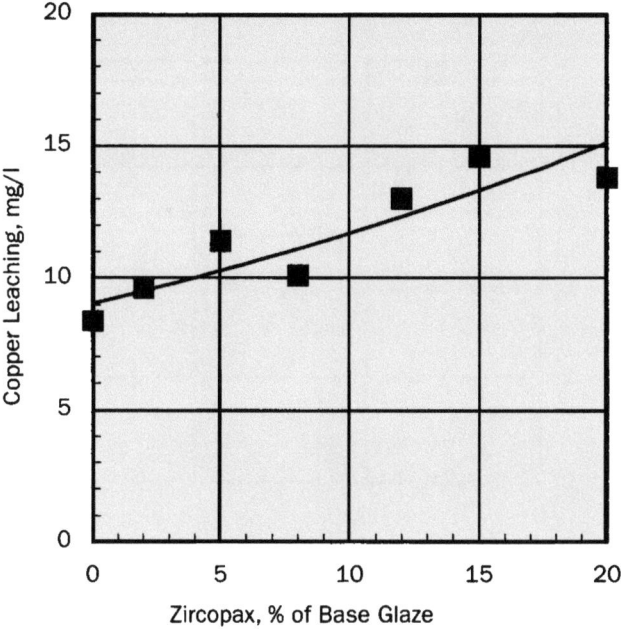

Figure 4-5. The effect of zirconium silicate on leaching of copper from a glaze.

170). Our advice as we write this has to be to use only enough zircon to get the opacity you need. Perhaps additional data over the next few years will shed more light on this situation.

Rutile (impure titanium dioxide), on the other hand, seems to aid stability at moderate levels. Figure 4-6 shows that relationship in another carefully controlled experiment where only the rutile level was varied.

While this data is more scattered than we would like, there would appear to be a definite benefit to adding 4-10% rutile to a glaze. We have seen a similar effect in a number of less carefully controlled experiments, where we tested various glazes containing 5% copper carbonate and 0% and 6% rutile. In every single instance, the rutile-containing glaze leached less copper than did the rutile-free glaze. Since rutile often gives a desired aesthetic effect, this is a positive result.

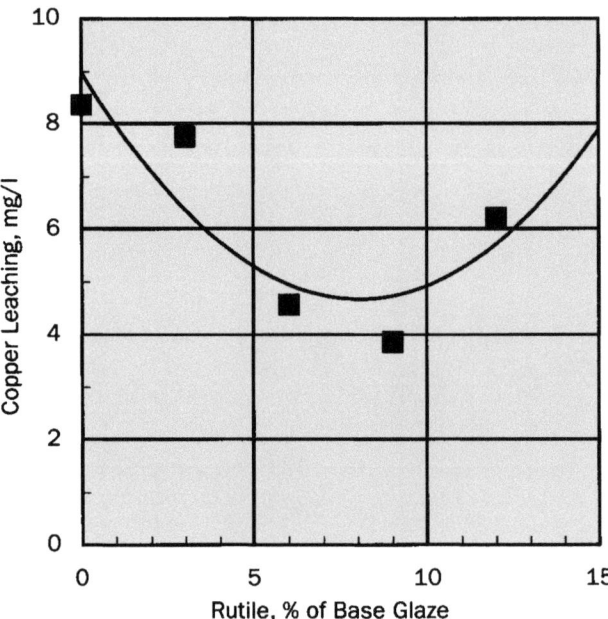

Figure 4-6. The effect of rutile level on leaching of copper from a glaze.

So those are the four rules. That's all we have at present, but we reserve the right to add more as we continue to learn. You can make very attractive glazes by staying within the rules and you will minimize your chances of making unstable glazes. You will see a selection of glazes we have developed using these rules in Chapter 6.

Guidelines for Improving Glaze Stability

We will present guidelines in three areas: 1) the types of fluxes 2) the balance of fluxes and 3) the level of boron. Our data supporting these guidelines is quite limited and we are drawing heavily on literature references to support the statements we make. What data we do have leads us to believe that following the guidelines will increase your odds of making a stable glaze. We know for certain there are stable glazes outside the guidelines and, in fact, have included some examples in Chapter 6.

Guideline 1

Favor alkaline earth materials or zinc oxide over alkalis when selecting fluxes. Soda, potash and lithia (alkalis) will generally hurt glaze stability while calcia, magnesia and strontia (alkaline earth materials) and zinc oxide will generally aid or at least not reduce stability. While some alkalis are in almost every glaze limiting their total concentration to about 25 % of the total fluxes (0.25 in the unity formula) seems a wise precaution. This is generally not difficult to do because higher levels normally result in thermal expansion/contraction rates that will cause crazing on many clay bodies.

Guideline 2

Favor a mix of fluxes vs. heavy dependence on just one or two. Perhaps another way to state this guideline is: stay within "limits" for fluxes. Examples of traditional limit formulas are given in Appendix I. This guideline seems to be less important than the other ones and we have violated it in the recipes we give in Chapter 6. For example, our high-calcium semimatte glazes are definitely outside traditional limits. However these glazes have been shown to be very stable in numerous leaching tests.

Guideline 3

Use enough boron to get thorough melting with the fluxes, alumina level and silica level you have chosen to use. In other words, use boron to assure you follow Rule 3. Erring on the side of having too much boron does not seem to have a significant negative effect on glaze stability, although it can dramatically affect the glaze aesthetics you are trying to achieve.

As our own experience grows with applying these rules and using or ignoring the guidelines, our confidence grows that the statements we have made above to describe their importance are accurate. We can summarize some of what we have said as follows: If you want to make a stable glaze, **always** follow the 4 Rules. If you want to make a glossy, stable glaze also follow the guidelines. If you want to make a stable semimatte or matte glaze go outside the guidelines cautiously.

What about Limit Formulas?

"Limit formulas" are sets of numbers derived by various researchers in the field of glaze chemistry that purport to establish ranges for the variety of oxides in a glaze (nearly always expressed in Seger unity formula terms) that will result in a balanced and stable glaze. They are always printed with the caution that they are only guidelines and should not be used by rote. They can be found in many books, among them Cooper and Royle (page 91), Zakin (pages 126-127), Green (page 118) and McKee (pages 35-37). Limit formulas are also integrated into at least some of the glaze calculation programs. A listing of two sets of limit formulas the authors believe are best is given in Appendix I.

It is important to understand how these limit formulas were developed. Almost without exception they were derived by taking a group of glaze recipes that were known, by visual observation or testing of specific properties like scratch resistance, to give "good glass" and analyzing them in Seger unity formula terms. They were undoubtedly then adjusted to include the judgement and experience of the person developing them. At the time most of them were derived there was no easy way to analyze leaching performance and whatever leaching evaluation, if done at all, was done only on lead-based glazes. That said, staying within limit formulas will yield stable glazes

A comment from John who did most of the stability testing for this book: "I know how to make an unstable glaze within so-called 'limits'. It is not too hard to find a set of fluxes, alumina and silica within limits that will not completely melt (thereby violating Rule 3). However, I don't yet know how to make an unstable glaze if I have followed the 4 rules."

a high percentage of the time provided those glazes are not overloaded with colorants or opacifiers. Stable glazes can be made outside of limits and unstable glazes can be made within limits. In addition, limit formulas are somewhat confining when it comes to aesthetic options. They tend to result primarily in glossy or semiglossy glazes. Some of those authors who propose limits for matte or semimatte glazes are clearly extending into the realm of 1) less-than-thoroughly-melted glazes or 2) low silica glazes with the limits they propose. In other words they are violating Rules 1 or 3 and will not have stable glazes by the meaning of the term in this book.

Overall, it is our opinion that the 4 "Rules" are more certain to give stable glazes and certainly will result in greater aesthetic choice. The downside of the "Rules" is that they give no guidance on the choice of specific flux combinations; however it is by allowing maximum flexibility on flux combinations that a wider variety of aesthetics is achievable.

Summary

It is not difficult to make stable or durable glazes. Following 4 easy-to-remember rules will almost always result in high quality glazes. Perhaps what is surprising to many people is that you can make stable glazes and still have a wide range of aesthetic options available to you. For whatever reason, it has been assumed by many people that stable glazes are boring glazes. This is simply not true! We would speculate that this belief has become commonly held because people have defined "stable glazes" and "glazes within limits" as being synonymous terms. Thinking in terms of the four rules should gradually change this misconception.

In Chapter 6 we will show you some glazes that any potter would want to have in their portfolio. There are very few glaze aesthetics that would otherwise be considered a desirable glaze on a functional surface that cannot be achieved in a stable framework. For that matter, nearly the same statement could be made about glazes intended for decorative or non-functional purposes.

5

FITTING GLAZES TO YOUR CLAY BODY

Understanding Crazing, Dunting and Shivering

This chapter addresses the problem of fit management—an important part of making ware stable and functional—by offering a way to assess the expansion/contraction rates of your clays and glazes.

Every clay/glaze/slip combination presents an opportunity to improve ware in terms of fit balance. We will provide a means of assessing the particular expansion rates of your clays and glazes which will lead to a better overall product.

Clay glaze fit, simply described, is the difference in size and hence strain between the clay and glaze or clay and glaze slip as they cool. Until a glaze becomes solid during cooling there is no problem. The glaze—being molten—simply adjusts perfectly to the contracting clay. Our materials contract on cooling and expand on heating. When the cooling glaze becomes rigid it can no longer adjust itself to the contracting body—no two bodies or glazes ever contract on cooling in exactly the same way.

There are special bodies and glazes that are developed to contract very little during cooling and expand very little on heating. There are even clays and glazes that have a negative expansion on heating and the opposite on cooling—they do not concern us here as all of our glazes contract on cooling and expand on heating.

The amount of expansion and contraction is what concerns us but, by themselves, these amounts are not the main problem—it is the difference in these rates between glaze, clay and slips which is of interest to us.

So now we have two or more materials bonded together but contracting, during cooling, at different rates. Either the glaze contracts more than the clay, less than the clay or exactly the same. It never happens that they are exactly the same because of the different natures of clays and glazes. This will be obvious when you see measurement charts of both materials.

Crazing

If the glaze contracts more than the clay, i.e. it becomes too small for the clay it is on, we can easily see the result—it crazes. This is because the glaze is being stretched and has to break apart. This is also called a glaze under tension; it is literally being pulled apart by the clay to which it

> Crazing glazes need a lower coefficient of expansion rate.

is bonded. Some potters like the effect and call it a crackle glaze; however, there are problems associated with this fault and they can damage your sales. For example:

1. When a glaze cracks it also starts a crack in the clay underneath it. This weakens the ware and it is more easily broken. If you try to "ring" a glazed stoneware or porcelain pot and it will not ring you may be sure it is either cracked or crazed.

2. The cracks in the glaze will eventually fill with discoloring material and the crazing will change the look of the ware. Some will see this as unsanitary. Many health departments will not allow restaurants to use crazed dinnerware. Keep in mind that in many cases crazing can happen weeks, months and even years after the ware comes out of the kiln. It's not usually considered to be a nice surprise by your customers.

3. A crazed surface is more vulnerable to chemical attack from acids or alkalis because there is more surface area to be attacked.

Shivering or Dunting

If the glaze winds up too big for the clay it is more difficult to see except when the difference is excessive and we get shivering and dunting. In this instance the glaze is under compression—it's being pushed together by the clay. If we have the "right amount" of compression we can make glazes that never craze and in fact make our ware stronger.

> Shivering/dunting glazes need a higher coefficient of expansion rate.

If the degree of compression is too high small slivers of razor sharp glaze can pop off rims and high points. Imagine how your customers feel when they find this happening. This is a very serious and dangerous glaze fault. The same kind of over compression of glaze can result in dunting—cracking of ware because the inside glaze won't let the clay contract properly during cooling. A typical scenario would be: low expansion glazes on the inside of a tea pot, hot water is poured in and the pot breaks. Sometime it takes a week, sometime a year, but it's always the same problem. The glaze was too big for the pot.

If the inside glaze is too big—and the outside glaze is too small—the pot will break more easily because the crazing glaze on the outside has already started the cracking process.

As you can see, low expansion glazes can be very problematic—certainly worse than crazing. We will show you how to test for both problems and how to avoid both.

> While dunting can often be alleviated by changing the clay body, we only recommend this approach if all or several of your glazes have fit problems. If only one or two glazes have fit problems it is usually easier to modify those glazes.

Determining Clay/Glaze Fit for Your Materials

In the material that follows, you will find five glazes having different coefficients of expansion that, for most of us, will cover the entire range we will experience. These glazes will help you find the calculated coefficient of expansion where gloss glazes will not craze on each of your clay bodies.

Matte glazes are not predictable by calculation. This is because matte glazes rely on crystals for the non-reflective or matte effect. Crystal formation is not quantitatively predictable and therefore calculation does not work. However, we can still measure matte glazes and get reliable information.

We will provide actual measurements of the expansions of these glazes along with the calculated expansions from some of the popular glaze calculation programs. If one of these pilot glazes fits your clay particularly well, you may find it to be useful as a base glaze—leach testing results are also provided using our standard additive package of 5% $CuCO_3$ and 6% rutile.

Understanding Dilatometer Measurements

The actual measurements of coefficient of expansion are done on a dilatometer such as the one shown in Figure 5-1. A dilatometer is an electronic machine which measures the expansion of clays and glazes as they are heated in a controlled environment. The ceramics industry would be lost without such information, but dilatometers are very expensive so individual potters are not accustomed to seeing the results.

The following pages explain how to read a dilatometer chart and also provide some actual charts of the clays and glazes we have used. Once you see the actual recorded expansion graphs it becomes obvious how useful this technology is to anyone trying to make functional ware of any

As your work becomes larger in size the forces of expansion and contraction have more effect. So, for example, the same combination of clay and glaze that is not a problem on a small bowl can have a serious effect on a large platter.

Figure 5-1. One of the two dilatometers in Ron's studio.

kind. The same information is useful to those making sculptural or non-functional ware.

Figure 5-2 is a dilatometer chart of a stoneware clay fired to cone 6. The vertical scale marks the percent linear change in a clay sample as it is heated. The horizontal scale indicates the temperature.

Notice the sharp increase in expansion around 573°C (1063°F). This is due to the change in the crystalline form of SiO_2 from alpha to beta (when going up in temperature). When a clay cools this increase in size is exactly reversible every time. The free quartz changes from beta to alpha with a corresponding decrease in size. This inversion is helpful in keeping glazes under compression to avoid crazing. It is why adding silica to a body is one way to help eliminate crazing. Many lowfire glazes and even some cone 6 glazes do not become rigid (frozen) until after this inversion. In that case having free silica serves little purpose.

The next chart, Figure 5-3, is of a glaze—in fact it is for our high expansion glaze #5. Glaze charts are different because glazes are glasses. As

> There can be some confusion regarding the use of silica to solve crazing problems. Unmelted crystalline silica in a clay body will increase the amount of quartz inversion thereby giving a higher expansion/contraction body. Melted silica in a glaze will lower the coefficient of expansion/contraction of the glaze. Therefore adding silica to either the body or the glaze can reduce crazing.

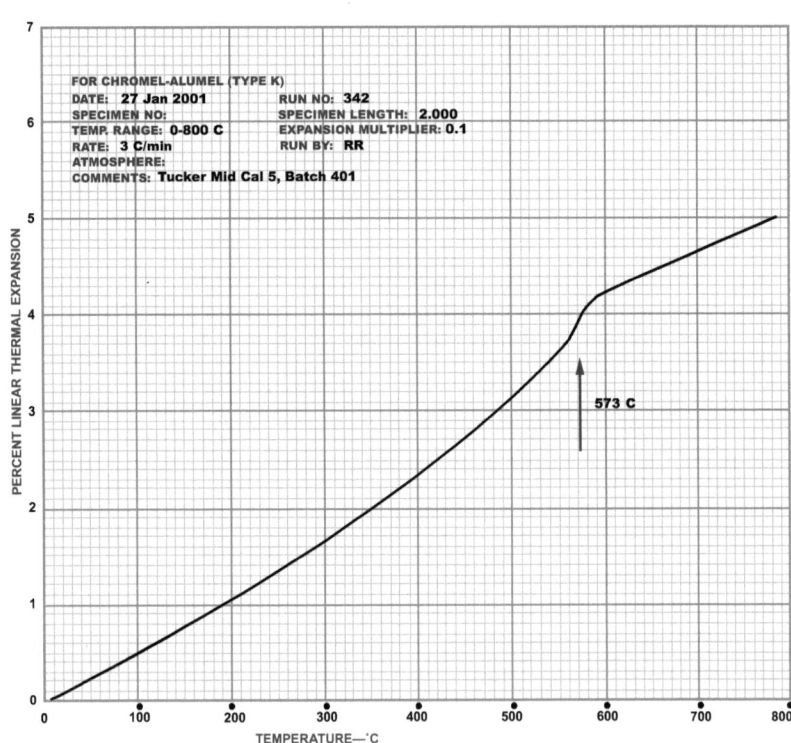

Figure 5-2. A dilatometer chart of Tucker Mid Cal 5 clay fired to cone 6. Curve repositioned to a standard starting point.

you can see there is no free quartz and, therefore, no inversion at 573°C (1063°F). What we do see is a relatively straight line up to the point at which the glaze starts to soften about 600°C (1112°F). Then the so-called

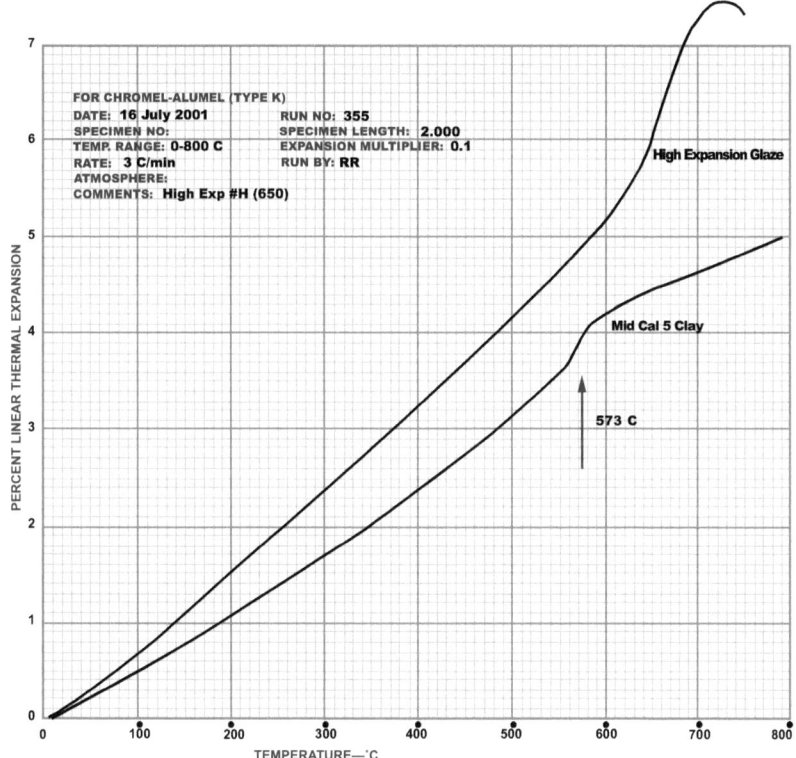

Figure 5-3. A dilatometer chart for a very high expansion glaze. Curves repositioned to standard starting point.

transition stage begins and, as you can also see, the rate of expansion increases dramatically. Glass needs to be carefully (evenly) cooled through this stage or it breaks. The temperature at which the line hooks over at the top is where the glaze has softened enough so that increase in size cannot register because the glaze is too soft. In other words the glaze is conforming to the forces being used to measure it and, in fact, it is shrinking. If we try to continue at this point the glaze becomes part of the measuring apparatus—definitely not what we want.

Figure 5-3 also shows the same line shown on Figure 5-2, the expansion curve for Tucker Mid Cal 5 clay, along with the high expansion glaze. This is a very useful way to compare clay and glazes—some glazes will fit well on some bodies and not on others. Just because a glaze fits well on the clay you are currently using does not mean it will work as well on any other clays. In this particular case, it is obvious that the glaze (top line) has a greater rate of expansion on heating and of contraction on cooling than the clay (bottom line.) This glaze will craze if it is put on this clay body. There is nothing you can do about that except to change either the glaze or the clay. This type of information would be very useful to potters who were trying to determine which other bodies would work well with their glazes. Unfortunately, many clay suppliers do not have or make available this kind of information.

Ideally we should have dilatometer charts of all our clays and glazes. We could then lay each glaze chart over each clay chart and immediately see which glazes would craze and which had a low enough expansion to present a shivering or dunting concern. How? As noted above, the slope of the dilatometer line for a glaze that will craze will be higher than the corresponding clay line. The reverse will be true for a glaze that will be under enough compression to either not craze, or if there is enough of a difference, to shiver and/or dunt.

Figure 5-4 shows the dilatometer information for the four clay bodies we used as we did the research for this book. As you can see they are quite similar to each other even though they represent a tan stoneware body and a porcelain body from each of two clay suppliers. We have kept the size of the charts the same so that you can trace a chart of the clay or glaze you wish to compare with other charts.

Since having glazes and clays measured in a dilatometer is very complex and more expensive than most potters can afford, we have developed a set of glazes to give you almost as good a gauge as an actual measurement for

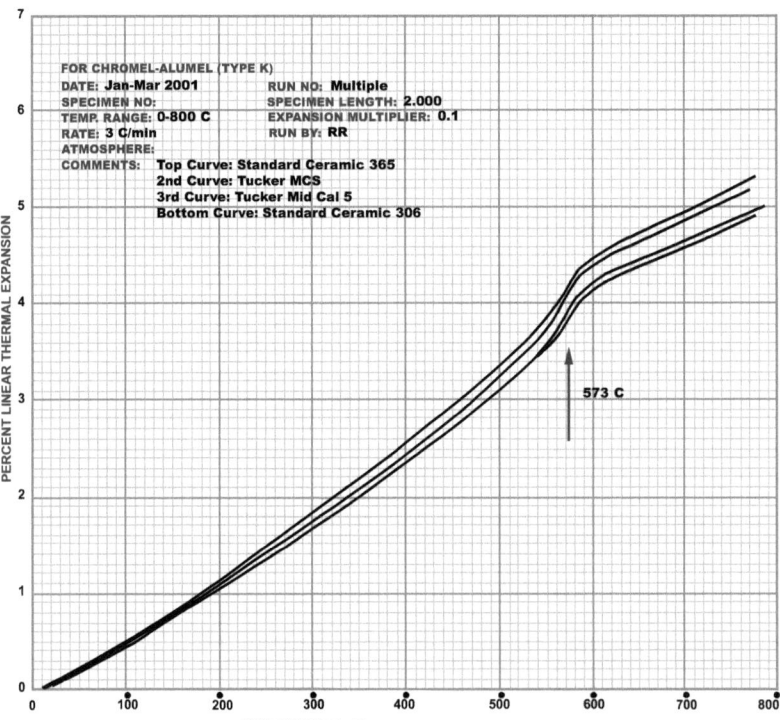

Figure 5-4. Dilatometer charts for the clay bodies used for the authors' research. Curves repositioned to standard starting point.

glossy glazes. The utility of this technique is, however, restricted to glossy glazes. As noted above, matte glazes which are composed of multiple phases, do not behave in as predictable a manner. For matte glazes, and in lieu of actual dilatometer charts, trial and error will have to do.

Expansion Test Glazes and How to Use Them

We have provided five glazes on the following pages which have a range of coefficients of expansion. Also given are their unity formulas and results of leach testing. By doing the experiments we outline below, you will find what glaze expansion/contraction is most appropriate for your clay body. Knowing this you will then be able to use calculated expansion numbers from your glaze calculation program to determine whether or not a new glossy glaze is likely to fit your clay. You can also use this information to help "fix" a glaze that does not fit your clay body.

Glaze #1—Low expansion—this may shiver on some clays and should certainly not be used as a liner glaze unless well tested.

Glaze #2—Medium low—this is the glaze that will tend not to craze on most cone 6 bodies—certainly not on the bodies we have been working with.

Glaze #3—Medium expansion—will craze on many cone 6 bodies but may take some weeks or even months.

Glaze #4—Medium high—will craze on the majority of cone 6 bodies.

Glaze #5—High expansion—will craze on just about any cone 6 body.

In most cases you will only have to use the first three glazes: #1 (low), #2 (medium low) and #3 (medium). If you can't get #3 to craze then you will have to use #4 (medium high). If you can't get #4 to craze it would be very unusual. Glaze #5 is a last resort; it crazes on any body we have tested.

We recommend mixing at least 1000 grams of each glaze—weigh carefully and balance your scales first. Make sure you are not using contaminated materials—you certainly don't want to be getting false results at this stage. Sieve twice through an 80 mesh screen as explained in Chapter 2.

It is best to apply these glazes in thin, medium and double thicknesses. You will soon see that thick applications will show crazing sooner than thinner applications. Even if the thin application doesn't craze while the thick one does, we don't recommend use of that glaze. Application thickness is one of those more difficult-to-control aspects of studio pottery and you will probably regret the practice.

In a normal firing, test each glaze on each of the clays you use. Remember, the bigger the test piece the faster fit problems will show up.

> Glossy glazes often consist of only one phase–a single glassy phase. Other glazes such as matte or semimatte glazes usually consist of multiple phases, e.g. crystals surrounded by glass.

> We realize it will be difficult for those without access to the materials we have used and who do not use calculation software to duplicate glazes. We will be working with others in various parts of the world to develop copies of these glazes using locally available materials. If you find yourself in a position where you are unable to reproduce them we may be able to help you find ways to make and use equivalent glazes. If you want to contact us for help in doing this it is essential that you have the analyses of your local materials available.

The object is to find the first glaze—going from low expansion up to high expansion—that crazes. It is a good idea to keep any leftover glaze to use on any new clays you may want to test in the future.

As a last check, you should take the glaze that does not craze and make sure it will not craze later. There are several techniques to bring out delayed crazing. See Chapter 3 for our recommendations on testing.

Once you have found the glaze that does not craze you have a reference point, but only for the clays and slips you have tested. Simply enter the recipe of that glaze in your calculation program and the calculated expansion will be a useful reference for choosing and making other glazes.

We must again stress—make sure your analyses are good for the materials you are using. Some software authors have included less than accurate and/or outdated analyses for the materials in their programs. For example, in some cases the analyses are theoretical (such as for feldspars) rather than actual mine analyses. Ask your clay supplier for the name, address and phone number of the mine—also get a lot number for the material if it is available—and contact the mine directly for a current analysis for each material you use.

A final recommendation is in order to assure successful results from this kind of clay/glaze fit testing. Some clay bodies are not properly vitrified at the firing temperature specified by their manufacturer. This is particularly so when a manufacturer specifies a wide firing range such as from cones 4 to 10. You can be almost certain that somewhere in that range the clay body will be less than properly vitrified and at some higher temperature it may be over-vitrified and brittle. A clay that is under-vitrified means water will eventually get into the clay and the body will expand enough to craze your glaze. There are many reasons not to use such clay bodies and delayed crazing is only one of them. Other reasons include unacceptable performance in a microwave, increased susceptibility to chipping, leaking of liquids and more. In addition to the testing we have outlined above always confirm that the water absorption for your fired clay is no higher than 3% and, preferably 1-2%. See Chapter 3 for instructions on how to measure water absorption.

If you want more precise information about your "magic" number (the expansion coefficient below which glazes will not craze on your clay body) you can combine the test glazes. Doing a volumetric line blend is good enough; see Chapter 7 for instructions if you are not familiar with volumetric line blending.

Interpreting Calculated and Measured Expansion Numbers

To this point in the text, we have avoided using specific numbers for coefficients of expansion. As we move into talking about the glazes we have developed for measuring clay/glaze fit, these numbers become very important. This is a confusing issue because you will find significant variation in reported expansion values for clay and glazes depending on which software program has been used or whether the numbers are from actual dilatometer measurements. This happens for several reasons. First, calculated expansion depends on the values determined for each individual oxide and there are several sets available in the published literature to choose from. The set the author of your particular glaze calculation software has chosen to use will affect the specific numbers you get. For the set of individual oxide expansion coefficients we prefer to use, see the side-bar associated with glaze #3. Second, calculated numbers are estimated using an algorithm called "the rule of mixtures". While this algorithm gives numbers that are directionally correct, it is an oversimplification of a very complex system. Third, the calculated numbers depend on having accurate material analyses. In all of the numbers we show, the material analyses have been updated to match the materials actually used. If you were to use material analyses numbers that came with your glaze calculation program you may not match our calculated numbers for the same recipe. The absolute coefficient of expansion numbers can only be accurately determined by actually measuring them with a dilatometer.

As if the above reasons were not enough, another reason coefficient of expansion numbers are confusing is that the various authors who have published on the subject use different ways of presenting the numbers. Let's take the number 0.00000493/°C as an example. This number represents the fractional change in length per degree Celsius increase in temperature and could be from an actual measurement or could be calculated by a glaze calculation program. We don't want to have to write that number out each time so we use a system to shorten it.

If we say ACE (average coefficient of expansion) is 4.93×10^{-6}/°C we have simply moved the decimal point 6 places to the right. If we say 493.0×10^{-8} we have moved the decimal point 8 places to the right. Some people, in more informal communications, will even use a shorthand notation and just present this number as 493 without the information on where the decimal point belongs. They are all the same number presented in different ways.

The net results of all this are sets of numbers like those shown on the following pages and summarized in Table 5-1. Note that in every case in Table 5-1, the calculated and actual measured expansion/contraction numbers from glaze to glaze are good indicators of higher or lower expansion.

Calculated/Measured Coefficients of Expansion
(Complete units omitted here; they are given on the following pages)

Glaze	Insight RR MDT**	Insight Orig. MDT**	HyperGlaze™	Measured* (50-600°C)
1 (Low)	348.92	6.41	64.84	5.40
2 (Med-Low)	424.79	7.02	71.05	5.78
3 (Medium)	501.51	7.56	76.69	6.36
4 (Med-High)	578.77	8.12	82.34	6.89
5 (High)	654.50	8.64	88.56	7.56

* The measured numbers above are averaged from calculated points on the dilatometer charts: Expansion = % linear change times multiplier (0.1) divided by [temperature minus starting temperature] times 1000.

** RR MDT and Original MDT refer to the materials databases used to supply compositions and expansion numbers to the program.

Table 5-1. Some examples of the different numbers that are calculated or reported for the same coefficient.

Consistency is the key to avoiding confusion. If possible, pick one software program and stick with it. If you must use different sets of expansion numbers when calculating you should make a conversion chart so you can compare the different reported/calculated coefficients of expansion. It will be easy to make a conversion chart by using our glazes which follow. Simply calculate our glazes using whatever software program you are used to and compare the expansions with those we provide. You will soon begin to tell which expansions are high or low or just right for your particular situation.

Are Calculated Expansion Numbers Useful?

It is important to note that all five of the test glazes on the following pages were designed using glaze calculation software. The design criteria were chosen to have approximately equal spacing between the **calculated** expansion coefficients. How well did we do versus what we actually measured with the dilatometer? Can glaze calculation software provide fairly accurate estimates of the relative expansion/contraction characteristics of glossy glazes? We think you will find the answer in Table 5-1 and Figure 5-5.

The calculated and the measured expansion numbers in Table 5-1 are well spaced apart. In Figure 5-5 we demonstrate this graphically by superimposing the dilatometer curves from glazes #1, #3 and #5 on the same graph. As you can see, they are also well spaced apart in roughly equal increments. We conclude glaze calculation software can be used to predict relative expansion of glossy glazes.

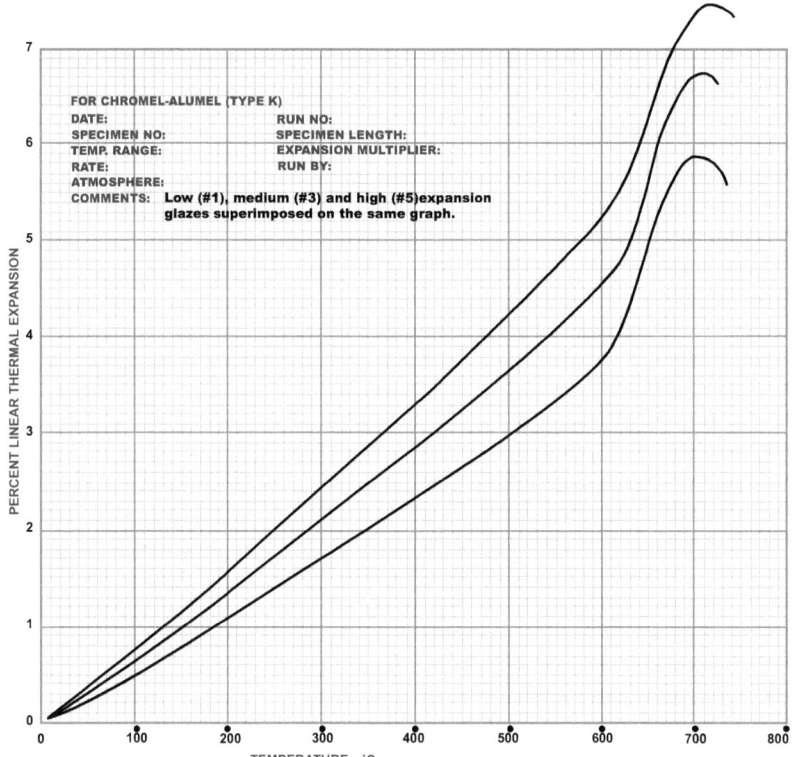

Figure 5-5. Dilatometer curves for expansion glazes #1, #3 and #5 superimposed on the same graph. Curves repositioned to standard starting point.

With that rather lengthy introduction, the next ten pages contain information on the glazes we have developed to help you learn how to best fit glazes to your clay(s).

Expansion Test Glazes

Glaze #1–Low Expansion

Glaze Recipe

Ferro Frit 3134	29.0
G-200 Feldspar	9.0
Talc	10.0
Wollastonite	4.0
EPK	22.0
Silica	<u>26.0</u>
Total	100.0

Comments:
1. Copper leaching with 5% copper carbonate and 6% rutile: 2.49 mg/l
2. To make an essentially equivalent glaze using Custer Feldspar instead of G-200, increase EPK to 22.5 and reduce silica to 25.5

Unity Formula

Fluxes

K_2O	0.038
Na_2O	0.183
CaO	0.516
MgO	0.263

Stabilizers

Al_2O_3	0.337
B_2O_3	0.330
Fe_2O_3	0.001

Glass Formers

SiO_2	3.606
TiO_2	0.003
Si:Al	10.7:1

> Pay special attention to our recommended firing rates—fast firing and cooling can give a false reading. Be sure to slow down as you approach maturity in a glaze firing and allow at least a 15 minute soak at peak temperature. This gives glazes a chance to establish a good bond with the clay. Weakly bonded glazes can be very difficult to keep in fit—the margin for success is very small compared to properly fired ware. Poorly bonded glazes shiver more easily—a very dangerous situation which you want to avoid at all costs.

This glaze has the lowest expansion/contraction of the five glazes. It will not craze on the majority of cone 6 bodies used by studio potters. If it is the only glaze in the series that does not craze on your clay, run a 5-part line blend with the medium-low expansion glaze (#2) to find a more accurate point where crazing stops. You can find an example of how to run a 5-part line blend towards the end of Chapter 7.

Note that this glaze (and most Cone 6 glazes) begins to soften a little above 600°C (1112°F). At 700°C (1292°F) it has softened to the point it begins to flow. Most of the "action" in the area of clay/glaze fit takes place below 600°C (1112°F) where the glaze has solidified to the point it can no longer adjust to differences in expansion/contraction rates between clay and glaze. That is why we quote average expansion coefficients over the range of 50-600°C (122-1116°F).

Fitting Glazes to Your Clay Body

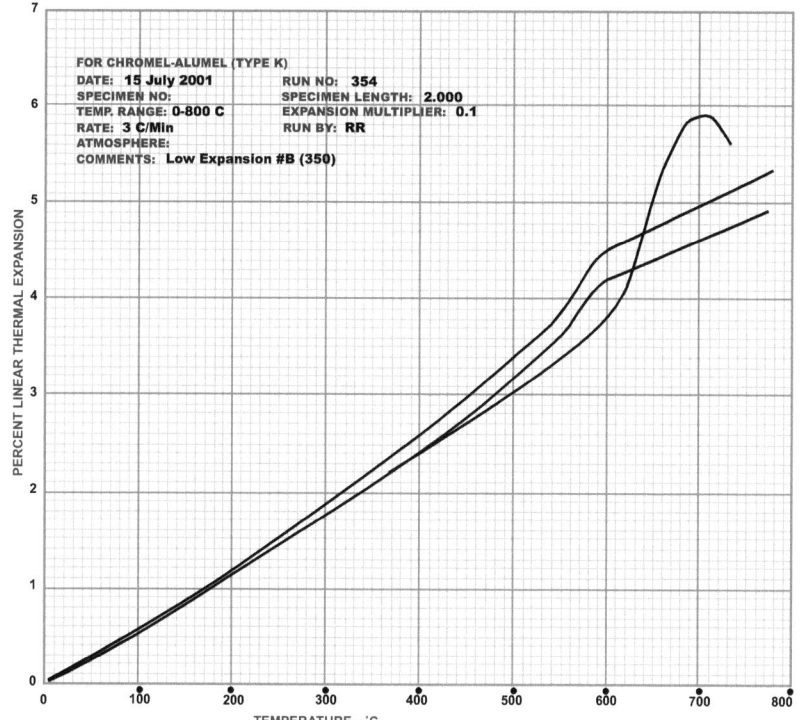

Figure 5-6. The dilatometer curve for low expansion Glaze #1. Curves repositioned to standard starting point.

Calculated Expansion Coefficients

Insight using RR's MDT	348.92 x 10^8/°C
Insight using original MDT	6.41 x 10^6/°C
HyperGlaze	64.84 x 10^7/°C

Measured Expansion Coefficient

At 50-600°C	5.40 x 10^6/°C

Set Point/Softening Point, °C

620/730

Figure 5-6 shows two reference curves in addition to the dilatometer curve for Glaze #1–namely, the dilatometer curves for the highest and lowest expansion clays that we used. Note that the glaze curve has a lower slope (expansion coefficient) than either clay curve until the glaze starts to soften at about 600°C (1112°F). This glaze will not craze on any of our 4 clays; however it is far enough under the curve for Standard Ceramic 365 (a grolleg porcelain) that it might shiver or cause dunting on that body. As noted earlier, this glaze should not be used as a liner glaze on Cone 6 bodies unless it has been very carefully tested for resistance to shivering and/or dunting.

> It would be desirable to be able to predict whether or not clay/glaze fit problems will occur by measuring the spacing between the dilatometer lines. Unfortunately it depends on too many factors for which we do not have complete understanding and is not possible to do at this time.

Glaze #2–Medium-Low Expansion

Glaze Recipe

Ferro Frit 3134	26.0
G-200 Feldspar	21.5
Talc	7.5
Whiting	5.5
EPK	20.0
Silica	<u>19.5</u>
Total	100.0

Comments:
1. Copper leaching with 5% copper carbonate and 6% rutile: 3.37 mg/l

Unity Formula

Fluxes

K_2O	0.085
Na_2O	0.182
CaO	0.543
MgO	0.191

Stabilizers

Al_2O_3	0.377
B_2O_3	0.290
Fe_2O_3	0.004

Glass Formers

SiO_2	3.315
TiO_2	0.003
Si:Al	8.8:1

> Expansion/contraction numbers from the actual measurement by dilatometer should be consistent from machine to machine. However this is not always so for a number of reasons. The annealing process the samples go through has a bearing, the rate of heating has an effect and each dilatometer has to have the calibration checked on a regular basis.

Next in our series of glazes is one with medium low expansion. Notice, in the unity formula, that we have achieved this mainly by doing two things. First, we have reduced the level of magnesium, a low expansion material, and replaced it with calcium, a moderate expansion material. Second, we have lowered the level of silica—another low expansion material. These are the same kind of substitutions you might want to make if you needed to raise the coefficient of expansion in a glaze to get out of a dunting or shivering problem.

Notice that this glaze has distinctly different performance than Glaze #1 when compared to the two referenced clay bodies. Its dilatometer curve is still well underneath Standard Ceramic 365 and, therefore, it will not craze on that body. Starting at the higher temperature and observing what happens as the clay and glaze cool, note that the glaze has solidified at about 620°C (1148°F) and from there down to 500°C (932°F) its contraction is lower than that of the Standard Ceramic 306 clay body which is going through its silica phase change from beta to alpha form. This means that at 500°C (932°F) the glaze is under compression. However from 500°C

Fitting Glazes to Your Clay Body

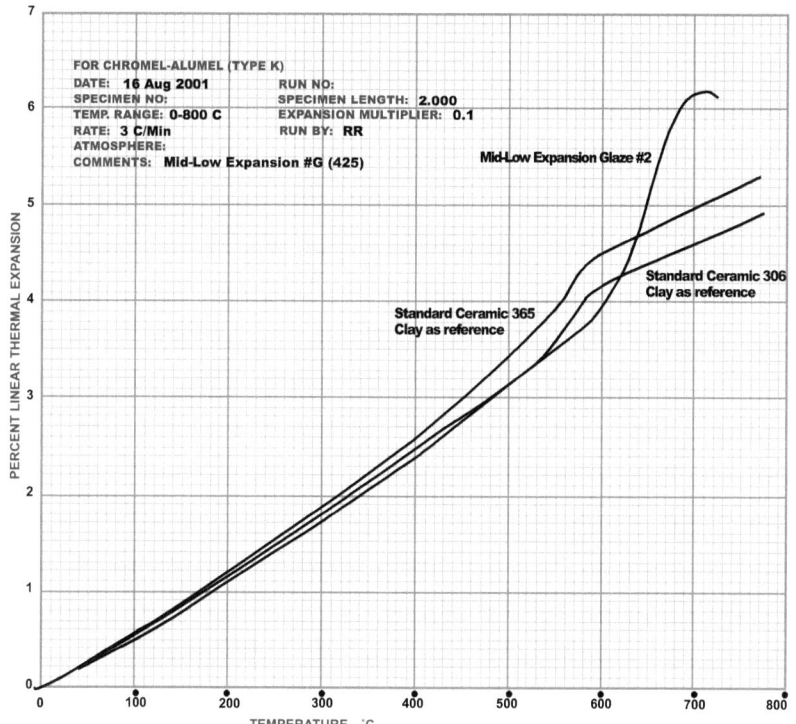

Figure 5-7. The dilatometer curve for mid-low expansion Glaze #2. Curves repositioned to standard starting point.

Calculated Expansion Coefficients

Insight using RR's MDT	$424.79 \times 10^8/°C$
Insight using original MDT	$7.02 \times 10^6/°C$
HyperGlaze	$71.05 \times 10^7/°C$

Measured Expansion Coefficient

At 50-600°C	$5.78 \times 10^6/°C$

Set Point/Softening Point, °C

620/730

(932°F) down to room temperature the glaze line is on top of the 306 line. Will the stretching of the glaze that occurs below 500°C be enough to overcome the compression that occured above that temperature? Will this cause the glaze to craze? This one is a close call. It probably will not craze, but it should be checked very carefully if we planned to use this glaze on this particular clay body. It may be one of those situations where crazing occurs months or years after the pot was fired. The accelerated testing we outline in Chapter 3 should always be used to help identify these marginal clay/glaze fit situations.

Glaze #3–Medium Expansion

Glaze Recipe
Ferro Frit 3134	20.0
G-200 Feldspar	36.5
Whiting	8.5
Talc	5.0
EPK	18.0
Silica	<u>12.0</u>
Total	100.0

Comments:
1. Copper leaching with 5% copper carbonate and 6% rutile: 3.99 mg/l

Unity Formula

Fluxes
K_2O	0.140
Na_2O	0.171
CaO	0.561
MgO	0.128

Stabilizers
Al_2O_3	0.441
B_2O_3	0.221
Fe_2O_3	0.004

Glass Formers
SiO_2	3.152
TiO_2	0.002
Si:Al	7.2:1

These are the expansion rates Ron uses as derived by English & Turner and published by Bailey and Hewitt (see Bibliography). Those not covered (*) in the English and Turner set have been estimated from other published data.

	$\times 10^{-6}/°C$
BaO	14.0
CaO	16.3
MnO_2*	5.7
Li_2O*	7.45
MgO	4.5
K_2O	39.0
Na_2O	41.6
ZnO	7.0
Fe_2O_3*	10.4
TiO_2*	10.6
B_2O_3	-6.53
Al_2O_3	1.4
SiO_2	0.5
PbO	10.6
P_2O_5*	7.45
SnO_2*	3.65
ZrO_2	2.3
SrO*	13.5

Note that boron is shown with a negative expansion rate. The "anti-crazing" aspect of boron begins to diminish at about 12 weight per cent in a glaze.

The third glaze in our series takes another step up in expansion. Again we have achieved this primarily by a further reduction in magnesia—this time magnesia has been replaced mainly by potassium oxide which is a high expansion material—and another small reduction in the silica level.

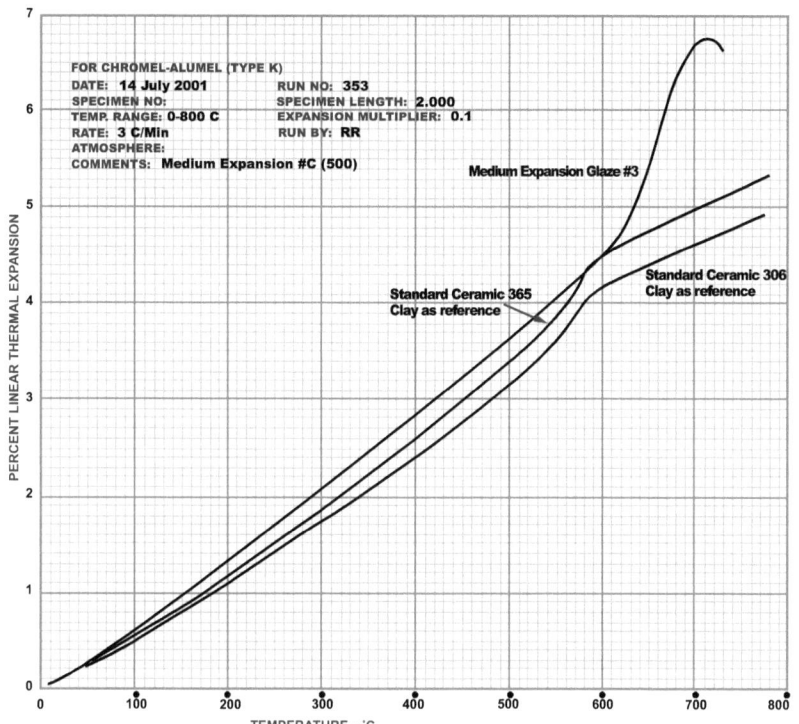

Figure 5-8. The dilatometer curve for the mid expansion glaze #3. Curves repositioned to standard starting point.

Calculated Expansion Coefficients

Insight using RR's MDT $501.51 \times 10^8/°C$
Insight using original MDT $7.56 \times 10^6/°C$
HyperGlaze $76.69 \times 10^7/°C$

Measured Expansion Coefficient

At 50-600°C $6.36 \times 10^6/°C$

Set Point/Softening Point, °C

640/740

This glaze also begins to soften (or completes solidification on cooling) at about 640°C (1184°F). Note that in the range of, say, 550°C (1022°F) down to room temperature its expansion coefficient (slope of the dilatometer line) is above both of the clays we have shown for reference. This means glaze #3 is very likely to craze on both clays, although it may take longer to craze on the higher expansion porcelain clay, Standard Ceramic 365.

Glaze #4–Medium-High Expansion

Glaze Recipe

Ferro Frit 3134	19.0
G-200 Feldspar	47.0
Whiting	12.0
Talc	2.0
EPK	10.0
Silica	<u>10.0</u>
Total	100.0

Comments:
1. Copper leaching with 5% copper carbonate and 6% rutile: 14.4 mg/l

Unity Formula

Fluxes

K_2O	0.168
Na_2O	0.170
CaO	0.612
MgO	0.050

Stabilizers

Al_2O_3	0.380
B_2O_3	0.197
Fe_2O_3	0.003

Glass Formers

SiO_2	2.914
TiO_2	0.001
Si:Al	7.7:1

In this glaze, we have modified the recipe by nearly eliminating talc which contains low expansion magnesium. Calcium plus the sum of sodium and potassium have been increased. Silica has also been reduced another step. This glaze would be expected to craze on most Cone 6 bodies and, indeed the dilatometer line in Figure 5-9 shows that it will. The glaze line is well above the lines representing the range of clay bodies we use.

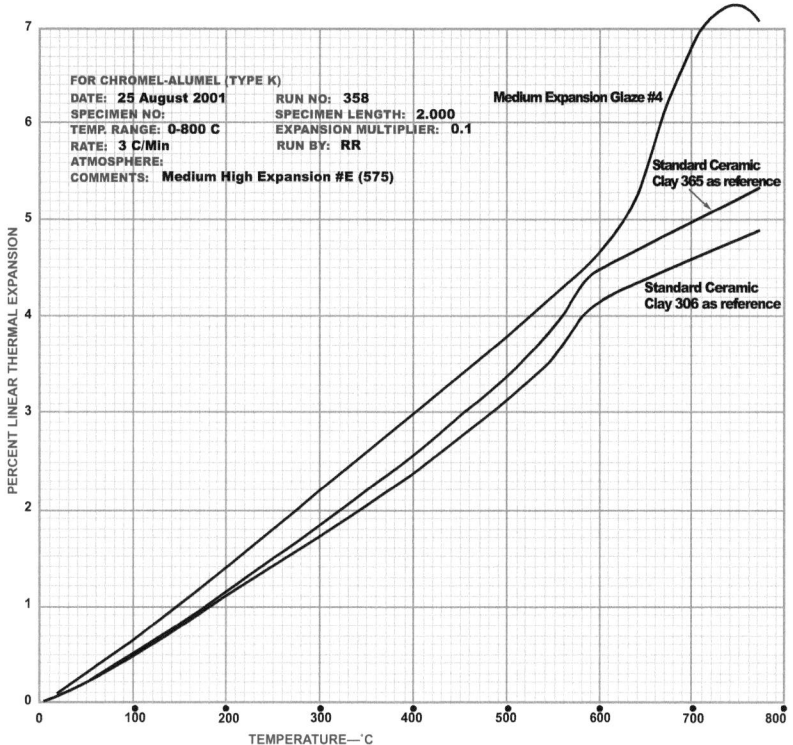

Figure 5-9. The dilatometer curve for medium high expansion glaze #4. Curves repositioned to standard starting point.

Calculated Expansion Coefficients

Insight using RR's MDT	$578.77 \times 10^{-8}/°C$
Insight using original MDT	$8.12 \times 10^{-6}/°C$
HyperGlaze	$82.34 \times 10^{-7}/°C$

Measured Expansion Coefficient

At 50-600°C	$6.89 \times 10^{-6}/°C$

Set Point/Softening Point, °C

620/730

Leaching performance has started to deteriorate with this glaze—it no longer meets our criteria for a general purpose base glaze, although it may have good leaching performance with moderate levels of colorants other than copper. This change in leaching performance vs Glaze #3 is probably due to slightly higher levels of sodium and potassium and slightly lower levels of silica and alumina.

Glaze #5–High Expansion

Glaze Recipe

Ferro Frit 3110	19.0
G-200 Feldspar	30.0
Whiting	13.5
Ferro Frit 3134	8.0
Strontium Carbonate	5.0
EPK	18.0
Silica	<u>6.5</u>
Total	100.0

Comments:
1. Copper leaching with 5% copper carbonate and 6% rutile: 18.6 mg/l. **We do not consider this glaze to be stable enough to use as a base glaze.**

Unity Formula

Fluxes

K_2O	0.117
Na_2O	0.223
CaO	0.556
MgO	0.004
SrO	0.101

Stabilizers

Al_2O_3	0.378
B_2O_3	0.100
Fe_2O_3	0.003

Glass Formers

SiO_2	2.565
TiO_2	0.002
Si:Al	6.8:1

The final glaze in our series has very high expansion. We have accomplished this by 1) nearly eliminating magnesia, 2) increasing soda and 3) decreasing silica and, therefore, silica-to-alumina ratio to about the minimum level in order to have reasonable stability and a glossy glaze. Although we say "reasonable" stability, this glaze does not meet our criteria for a good base glaze. It may be suitable in certain situations with low levels of non-copper-containing colorants.

Note how far above our clay lines this glaze dilatometer curve is. This glaze will craze almost immediately on nearly all commercial cone 6 bodies. While it might make a good crackle glaze for decorative work, we would not consider it to be a good glaze for functional pottery. In addition to its crazing propensity, this glaze did not do very well on our standard leaching test. This is probably because of the relatively high levels of sodium (necessary to get the high expansion) coupled with a minimal level of silica. Sodium is known to reduce chemical stability.

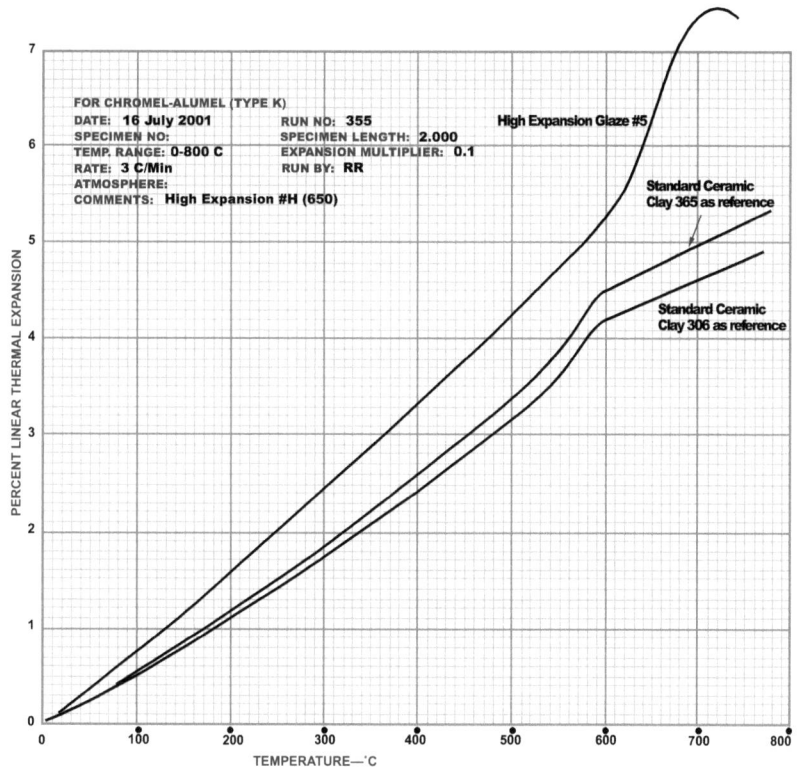

Figure 5-10. The dilatometer curve for the high expansion glaze #5. Curves repositioned to standard starting point.

Calculated Expansion Coefficients

Insight using RR's MDT	654.50 x 10^8/°C
Insight using original MDT	8.64 x 10^6/°C
HyperGlaze	88.56 x 10^7/°C

Measured Expansion Coefficient

At 50-600°C	7.56 x 10^6/°C

Set Point/Softening Point, °C

640/730

Summary

Achieving a good fit of clay and glaze is, admittedly, a time consuming, difficult task. However it is one we believe functional potters, in particular, must pay more attention to. The techniques we have outlined above should allow you to learn the approximate calculated coefficient of expansion that will result in a glaze fitting each of your clays. Use that number as a goal in future development of or choice of your glossy glazes. As in all the material presented in this book, however, your final glazes must be thoroughly tested by the procedures we outline in Chapter 3 to assure a satisfactory product.

We realize that our glazes are made with materials easily available in North America. We have provided the typical analysis for all these materials in Appendix F. If you have reliable analyses for the materials available to you it will often be possible to duplicate our glazes using a glaze calculation program. Remember—your calculations are only as good as your analyses so make sure they are right. Contact your supplier or, better still, contact the mine or manufacturer. Avoid materials you cannot get analysis for or else have them analyzed.

It is also possible for you to make your own set of test glazes using locally available materials. If you do so, aim for expansion rates in evenly graduated steps. Start with a glaze that does craze and lower the expansion in stages—sometimes it is simply a matter of adding silica. When that eventually results in a glaze that is no longer shiny (as it eventually will) adding a low expansion oxide like boron (B_2O_3) or magnesium (MgO) will further lower your coefficient of expansion.

Finally, in addition to helping you produce better fitting glazes for your pottery, working through the procedures presented in this chapter will certainly increase your knowledge of and comfort with coefficient of expansion numbers and calculations. As is often the case, actually working with a complex problem will increase your understanding of it manyfold.

****

"A stoneware potter sometimes tends to think that since the body of his ware is vitreous and non-porous, crazing is only a skin-deep and therefore a venial fault...But it has been proved that glaze fit has a major effect on strength. Small rods of porcelain, all made of the same process from the same body, are divided into three groups: some are dipped in a crazing glaze, some left unglazed, and others dipped in a sound glaze; all are then given the same firing treatment. The comparative strength after firing is in the proportions 40:100:160, indicating that the vitreous ware with a non-crazing glaze may be three or four times stronger than the ware which is crazed."

Michael Cardew, Pioneer Pottery

6

STONEWARE AND PORCELAIN GLAZES

Most of the glazes developed for this chapter originated in John's studio. He did the initial assessment of resistance to acids and the appearance of the glaze vs our aesthetic goals. When a glaze passed those initial screens it went under Ron's scrutiny. He examined the glaze recipe for things such as clay/glaze fit (crazing and shivering), pinholing, crawling, slurry stability in the bucket and more. Back and forth we went until we had a glaze that met both of our critical eyes. Some candidates were rejected at the 11th hour because we just couldn't get past one or another of our requirements. The resulting glazes are probably the most tested to be published by and for potters since the time when glaze developers were trying to learn how to make lead-based glazes stable in the early and mid-20th century. In doing this development work, we purposely limited ourselves to materials which are widely available and which have a reputation for consistent composition. Ron's input was particularly important here since he has been looking at mine analyses of materials for many years. It was exciting to be able to demonstrate that truly remarkable glazes could be formulated from "mundane" materials. We remain convinced that there is little need to work with unreliable or overly soluble materials such as Gerstley Borate or lithium carbonate to achieve beautiful and stable glazes. When you get down to the important facts, chemistry is chemistry and a molecule of boron oxide can be supplied equally well from a frit as it can from Gerstley Borate. Total composition is extremely important, of course, and you must take into account all of the components of a glaze if you are to achieve the effects you want. That is why nearly all of these glazes started as a set of numbers within a glaze calculation program. Those that didn't begin there were certainly adjusted and optimized with the help of a glaze calculation program.

As has been said throughout this book, our glazes are intended to be durable, trouble-free, reliable and reproducible. That does not mean that you can just throw things together in a sloppy manner or fire them any way your heart desires and get glazes that look like ours. If you hope to duplicate our results you must mix your glazes, apply them and fire your glazed pots with care. Good craftsmanship is required. If you don't know what we mean by that, reread Chapter 2.

You will also have to assure that the fit between the glaze and your clay body is good. We used clay bodies that should be representative of many of the commercial cone 6 stoneware and porcelain bodies; however, body expansion/contraction levels can vary over a wide range. The bodies we used and their expansion characteristics are documented in Chapter 5. Even then, there will be some difference between your results and ours due to natural variations in raw materials, differing thicknesses of application and differing firing profiles or conditions. For example, it is very important that you have the materials analyses for the particular materials that you are using. Check them against what we used (Appendix F) and make adjustments to match our unity formula calculations if necessary.

All of the above reasons illustrate why you must do your own testing and assure yourself that your finished product is suitable for the use for which it is intended. In those same paragraphs you will find several reasons why glaze recipes don't "travel" well between potters. We have done our best to use reliable, consistent ingredients and we have thoroughly documented our application and firing techniques. There are still a number of variables which only you can control or measure. We can't do that for you.

In addition to the above criteria, in selecting specific recipes we aimed for a wide range of surfaces and color responses. Several of our glazes will be presented as a **base glaze** with several color variants. You are invited to experiment with and find other colors that you find particularly attractive. These base glazes are the most stable we have found in their class. We tested these glazes colored with 5% $CuCO_3$ and 5-6% rutile and selected only those that leached less than 6 mg/l of copper. We have found that if a glaze will perform this well when tested with this high amount of copper, it will leach only tiny quantities of other colorants as long as the levels of those colorants are kept to reasonable amounts—see Chapter 4. Note that these glazes have been developed with aesthetics and performance as the sole criteria. We did not use minimum number of ingredients or easy-to-remember recipes as one of our goals.

We have also included some **specialty glazes**. These are glazes that either 1) failed our criteria above for designation as a base glaze, e.g. they may have leached up to 15-20 mg/l in our standards test with copper carbonate and rutile or 2) they may be more limited in their application for some other reason. In spite of this, they are extremely stable with the colorants shown and they represent color or surface variants we don't know how to get another way. If you do experiment with other variations of these specialty glazes we recommend you keep copper levels low and be extra cautious in evaluating their suitability for your particular application.

The tests we recommend in Chapter 3 have all been performed on at least one color variant for each base glaze. For example, leach testing has been done on all base glazes with 5% copper carbonate and 5-6% rutile added, although only on one clay body—normally a tan stoneware. In the limited leach testing we have done of glazes on a porcelain body the results were essentially identical to those obtained on a stoneware body. Nearly all of the colors shown have also been leach tested and the results are given. The entire battery of tests has not been done on each color variant. Again, you must perform your own tests to verify that your work meets your own standards or goals.

All of the glazes in this book have been developed for firing at Orton Cone 6. It is worth repeating what we mean by that. To us, cone 6 is achieved when a large, regular cone 6 is bent so that its tip is just touching the shelf or support on which it sits. A self-supporting cone will be bent to about 4-5 o'clock. Cone 7 will normally be just starting to bend. Cone 6 is definitely **not** when a small cone 6 in a Kiln Sitter® shuts the kiln down. We cannot state strongly enough that using a Kiln Sitter® to shut off your kiln and then letting it cool naturally is a surefire route to mediocre, at best, glazes. Depending on exactly how your Kiln Sitter® is calibrated, the shut-off point could be all the way from cone 4 to cone 9—it is very unlikely that it is cone 6! In addition, using a Kiln Sitter® to shut off the kiln will not allow you to soak at peak temperature for a few minutes or to cool slowly; both of which we highly recommend. With most kilns it is necessary to have cone packs in several places throughout to assure that you are firing evenly. Doing this will repay the small extra cost of the cones many times over as the years go by.

All of the glazes have also been developed in the oxidizing atmosphere of an electric kiln. Their performance in reduction is not known; although all except one (the zinc-based glaze) are potentially suitable for reduction firing. Any glazes containing significant amounts of iron (say more than 1%), if fired in reduction, must be checked carefully for running. Iron acts as a flux in reduction and can have a significant effect on whether or not the glaze stays on the pot.

One last point needs to be made with regard to the surface descriptions of our glazes. A glaze that is a semimatte with no additives may well be semiglossy or even glossy when, for example, 6% rutile and 5% copper carbonate are added. Sometimes it may even go in the other direction and become more matte. Colorants and opacifiers affect glazes, although by ignoring them in Seger unity calculations we are assuming they do not.

With that introduction, here are our glazes organized into the categories of base glazes and specialty glazes.

> One can, of course, override a Kiln Sitter® and turn the kiln back on to allow soaking at peak temperature or slow cooling. Although we realize many potters do this, it is not a practice we can recommend. We believe a Kiln Sitter's primary purpose is as a safety device and, as a matter of principle, safety devices should not be overridden. If you do choose to override, please exercise extreme caution and stay with the kiln at all times.

Base Glazes

High Calcium Matte/Semimatte Glazes

These glazes have evolved over 3-4 years to what is now a very attractive and stable pair of semimatte glazes. The two recipes presented are extremely close to each other and differ only a small amount in their level of matteness or glossiness. The first is slightly more matte—start with it if that is what you want—however neither is a dry matte. They are both in the range of matte to semimatte depending on the specific colorants and opacifiers that are added.

High Calcium Semimatte Base 1

Glaze Recipe		Unity Formula	
Ferro Frit 3195	20.0	*Fluxes*	
Wollastonite	29.0	K_2O	0.010
Nepheline Syenite	4.0	Na_2O	0.090
EPK	30.0	CaO	0.857
Silica	<u>17.0</u>	MgO	0.043
Total	100.0	ZnO	
		Stabilizers	
Comments:		Al_2O_3	0.488
1. Copper leaching with 5%		B_2O_3	0.226
copper carbonate and 6%		Fe_2O_3	0.007
rutile: 5.08 mg/l			
		Glass Formers	
		SiO_2	3.196
		TiO_2	0.004
		Si:Al	6.5:1

This glaze needs to be applied on the thin side. Thick coats, particularly when the glaze contains few or no colorants or opacifiers, can result in a few pinholes. It also must be cooled slowly (less than or equal to 80°C (150°F) per hour down to 800°C (1500°F) to allow recrystallization to occur, which is necessary for a nice semimatte surface. See Appendix E for an example of a firing cycle that works. If it is cooled rapidly this glaze can be quite glossy.

Three color variants of this glaze are shown on the following pages.

*Figure 6-1. **Variegated Slate Blue**. High Calcium Semimatte Base 1 with 6% rutile, 3% copper carbonate and 1.5% cobalt carbonate. Leaching of copper and cobalt respectively: 0.80 and <0.02 mg/l. This mug represents the more normal semimatte appearance of this glaze. See Figure 6-4 on the next page to see a different way of using this*

*Figure 6-2 (left). **Oatmeal**. High Calcium Semimatte Base 1 with 4% manganese dioxide and 6% rutile. Leaching of manganese: 0.06 mg/l. The rim has been dipped in a charcoal version of a similar base glaze.*

*Figure 6-3. **Field Mouse Brown**. High Calcium Semimatte Base 1 with 4% manganese dioxide, 0.4% cobalt carbonate and 6% rutile. Leaching of manganese and cobalt respectively: 0.06 and <0.02 mg/l.*

Figure 6-4. **Variegated Slate Blue.** High Calcium Semimatte Base 1 with 6% rutile, 3% copper carbonate and 1.5% cobalt carbonate (the same glaze as shown in Figure 6-1). This sake jar is showing quite a bit of gloss where it is thicker. This might have been more uniformly semimatte if we had cooled even more slowly; however we decided we liked it the way it was.

Here is the second version of our high calcium semimatte base glaze. Note that neither of these base glazes is within traditional "limit formulas"—both are on the high side with respect to calcium—but both are very stable to acid leaching and also perform well in the other tests we recommend. Limit formulas would say that the maximum calcium level should be about 0.6-0.65 and we are up to 0.85 with both of these glazes.

High Calcium Semimatte Base 2

Glaze Recipe

Ferro Frit 3195	23.0
Wollastonite	28.0
Nepheline Syenite	4.0
EPK	28.0
Silica	<u>17.0</u>
Total	100.0

Comments:
1. Copper leaching with 5% copper carbonate and 6% rutile: 5.54 mg/l

Unity Formula

Fluxes

K_2O	0.010
Na_2O	0.100
CaO	0.850
MgO	0.040
ZnO	

Stabilizers

Al_2O_3	0.478
B_2O_3	0.259
Fe_2O_3	0.006

Glass Formers

SiO_2	3.193
TiO_2	0.004
Si:Al	6.7:1

This glaze has a little less alumina and slightly more boron than High Calcium Semimatte Base 1. The net result is a glaze that is a little shinier. With most color variants, though, this glaze will still be in the semimatte or satin range. The same notes on application and firing apply to this glaze as to Base 1 above. The first two color variants below make use of only rutile and red iron oxide. Even though the one containing red iron oxide was leach tested for completeness, both would fit our definition of **liner** glazes as described in Chapter 1.

As you look at the glazes on the following 2 pages, notice how **Bone** looks very different on different bodies even though this is a relatively opaque glaze. Just adding iron oxide to the **Bone** glaze can give a very attractive **Raw Sienna**. Like **Variegated Slate Blue** (Figure 6-4) it also tends to be glossier where thick, and matte where thin. Although Raw Sienna could also be tried in reduction, expect very different results. Iron is a very active flux in reduction and this glaze may be "overfluxed" in that firing environment. With **Spearmint**, we show how copper carbonate and rutile combine to give a beautiful soft green.

*Figure 6-5. **Bone** on a porcelain sake jar and cup. High Calcium Semimatte 2 with 6% rutile. Not leach tested: contains nothing of concern. Note that the texture is not quite as noticeable and the color is clearly different than the same glaze on a tan stoneware body below.*

*Figure 6-6 (left). **Bone** on a stoneware sake jar. High Calcium Semimatte 2 with 6% rutile. Not leach tested: contains nothing of concern.*

*Figure 6-7. **Raw Sienna** on a stoneware sake jar. High Calcium Semimatte 2 with 6% rutile and 6% red iron oxide. Leaching of iron: 0.12 mg/l.*

Stoneware and Porcelain Glazes

*Figure 6-8. **Spearmint** on a porcelain sake jar. High Calcium Semimatte 2 with 4% copper carbonate and 6% rutile. Leaching of copper: 1.63 mg/l*

> In a side-by-side test with both glazes colored with 5% copper carbonate, 5% rutile and 5% Zircopax, 5-20s leached 10.95 mg/l of copper. Our general purpose **Glossy Base Glaze 1** leached only 1.28 mg/l. Results from this kind of testing can vary significantly; however, this spread is big enough that we conclude there is definitely a difference in resistance to acid leaching when the two glazes are heavily loaded with copper.

General Purpose Glossy Base Glazes

This glaze was derived from one of Tony Hansen's glazes—his so-called 5-20s (20% each of the ingredients below except for talc) glossy base glaze. It has been modified to improve the leaching performance. Although the original had fairly good performance and does quite well with many colorants, this glaze performs significantly better (see the side-bar). It can be used with no opacifier for a clear to translucent glaze or with an opacifier for opaque glossy colors. With no colorants or opacifiers at all it is slightly milky so we suggest using the glaze that follows later in this chapter that is designated as a liner glaze if you want a good, clear, glossy, liner glaze.

Glossy Base Glaze 1

Glaze Recipe		Unity Formula	
G-200 Feldspar	20.0	*Fluxes*	
Ferro Frit 3134	20.0	K_2O	0.074
Wollastonite	10.0	Na_2O	0.135
EPK	20.0	CaO	0.512
Talc	11.5	MgO	0.279
Silica	<u>18.5</u>	ZnO	
Total	100.0		
		Stabilizers	
		Al_2O_3	0.344
Comments:		B_2O_3	0.202
1. Copper leaching with 5% copper carbonate and 5% rutile: 1.28 mg/l		Fe_2O_3	0.004
		Glass Formers	
		SiO_2	3.163
		TiO_2	0.002
		Si:Al	9.2:1

> This glaze has expansion/contraction characteristics in between the low and medium/low glazes in Chapter 5. It should fit most Cone 6 bodies well.

This glossy glaze is relatively robust. Thickness of application is important when it is colored, as you will see in the photographs that follow; although thickness is less important as you add more and more colorants and/or opacifier to the glaze. This feature, of course, can be used to good aesthetic effect. We hope you will find it to be quite reliable.

In developing color variants for this glaze we focused on the blue family. After all, what functional potter does not need blue in his product line? Color variants of this glaze can be developed across a broad range.

In Figures 6-9 and 6-10, notice how striking the texture is on stoneware vs on porcelain. While this glaze breaks very nicely off texture, the contrast of the relatively light glaze breaking off the tan clay body is much more dramatic. You could also get a very nice effect by using dark slip for your accent on a porcelain body.

Stoneware and Porcelain Glazes

Figure 6-9. **Powder Blue** *on tan stoneware. Glossy Base Glaze 1 with 0.75% cobalt carbonate, 0.8% nickel oxide, 6.0% rutile, and 8% Zircopax. Leaching of cobalt and nickel respectively: <0.02 and <0.02 mg/l .*

Anytime we use the symbol "<", as we have in the above paragraph, it simply means that the amount of material which leached was less than the detectable limit of the analytical equipment we were using. The number that follows the "<" symbol is the detectable limit for the material of interest. If it were desired, smaller amounts of material could be detected with a more sensitive (and expensive) procedure.

Figure 6-10 (left). **Powder Blue** *on porcelain. Note how much less noticeable the texture is with this glaze on porcelain.*

Figure 6-11. **Clear Powder Blue** *on stoneware This is also the same glaze as in Figures 6-9 and 6-10 minus the Zircopax. Note how the glaze near the rim, which was double dipped, looks similar to the glaze in Figure 6-9, but the glaze on the body is significantly different with more body color showing through.*

Whether or not you use an opacifier, and which opacifier you choose, can make a big difference in a glaze. We have chosen to illustrate the use of zirconium silicate (trade names of Zircopax and Superpax) because of its lower cost vs another excellent opacifier, tin oxide. Even though you may have to use more zirconium its cost will still be substantially less. Some people prefer the softer look achieved with tin and if that is your goal feel free to experiment with it. You can also see the effect of opacifier vs no opacifier by looking at Figures 6-9 and 6-11.

Figure 6-12 shows the same **Glossy Base 1** with a different colorant combination. We've added a little copper carbonate to give a hint of green and a little red iron oxide to take some of the harshness out of cobalt blue. We've named this glaze **Variegated Blue**; again the rutile is having a significant effect. Remember that this is the same glaze shown in Chapter 2 where we illustrate how different it can look when applied more thinly and on a stoneware body.

Figure 6-12. **Variegated Blue** on a porcelain sake jar. Glossy Base 1 with 1.0% cobalt carbonate, 0.75% copper carbonate, 3% red iron oxide and 6% rutile. Leaching of cobalt and copper respectively: <0.02 and 0.183 mg/l.

The last glaze in this series is one we call **Bright Sky Blue**. Colored primarily with cobalt, we have put in rutile for a more mottled appearance and just a hint of red iron oxide to take the edge off the cobalt. It has a very nice feel to it that just makes you want to hold it. Testing glazes on a highly textured tile is an excellent way to see how much they move during firing. As you can see in Figure 6-13 Bright Sky Blue accentuates texture nicely.

Note also how different this glaze looks and behaves depending on whether it is on porcelain or stoneware. Not only is there a color difference due to the different colors of the substrates, but also the glazes interact with the clays differently because of the differing chemistry of the clay bodies. Cone 6 porcelain bodies always contain more flux (feldspar and/or nepheline syenite) and silica than stoneware bodies and some of that material may move into the glaze and result in more melting and glaze flow.

*Figure 6-13. **Bright Sky Blue** on tan stoneware. Glossy Base 1 with 1.0% cobalt carbonate, 6.0% rutile and 0.5% red iron oxide. Leaching of cobalt: <0.02 mg/l.*

*Figure 6-14 (left). **Bright Sky Blue** on tan stoneware.*

*Figure 6-15. **Bright Sky Blue** on porcelain.*

Glossy Base Glaze 2

This glaze was first introduced as a glossy black glaze called Ron Roy Black on Clayart more than 2 years ago. It has been thoroughly tested by several people and found to be very stable and reliable. The only debate has revolved around whether or not it was true black. The original version contained 9% red iron oxide and 1% cobalt carbonate as its colorants and some people (Ron's coauthor included) found this to be slightly on the brown side of black. Adding another percent cobalt carbonate seems to have done the trick without affecting acid stability in any significant way.

As we were testing glazes for this book, however, we tested this glaze with our usual 5% copper carbonate and 6% rutile. It tested very well as noted in the table below. So while we present it in its black version, now renamed Licorice as shown in Figure 6-16, please feel free to experiment with other colors. This glaze will also make an excellent clear liner glaze along with the glaze that follows which is specifically designated as a liner glaze.

Licorice is about as trouble-free as a glaze gets. It is not particularly sensitive to thickness of application and seems to have virtually no faults in the testing we have done. It is an excellent basic glossy black and may be best used accented with another glaze.

> This glaze has expansion/contraction characteristics slightly higher than Glossy Base Glaze 1, but in the same range. It should fit most Cone 6 bodies well. The same is true of the glaze on the opposite page.

Glossy Base Glaze 2

Glaze Recipe		Unity Formula	
Ferro Frit 3134	26.0	*Fluxes*	
Custer Feldspar	22.0	K_2O	0.094
Talc	5.0	Na_2O	0.210
Whiting	4.0	CaO	0.548
EPK	17.0	MgO	0.147
Silica	<u>26.0</u>	ZnO	
Total	100.0		
		Stabilizers	
Comments:		Al_2O_3	0.386
1. Copper leaching with 5% copper carbonate and 6% rutile: 0.93 mg/l		B_2O_3	0.335
		Fe_2O_3	0.004
2. To use G-200 Feldspar instead of Custer, reduce EPK to 16.0 and increase silica to 27.0		*Glass Formers*	
		SiO_2	4.120
		TiO_2	0.002
		Si:Al	10.7:1

A Clear, Glossy Liner Glaze

Some potters prefer to have a clear glaze on the inside of ware such as mugs, pitchers and bowls and, in fact, some buyers of pottery seem to prefer that also. This glaze should meet that need for most Cone 6 stoneware and porcelain clays. Even though we recommend it as a clear glaze, it has been leach tested with our usual 5% copper carbonate and rutile. Its leaching performance is quite good and it meets our standards for a base glaze, and is more transparent than **Glossy Base Glaze 1**.

Figure 6-16. **Licorice** *on tan stoneware. Glossy Base Glaze 2 with 9% red iron oxide and 2% cobalt carbonate. The rim of this mug has been overdipped with* **Waterfall Brown** *that is shown later in this chapter. Leaching of cobalt: <0.02 – 0.07 mg/l in numerous tests.*

Glossy Clear Liner Glaze

Glaze Recipe	
G-200 Feldspar	20.0
Ferro Frit 3134	20.0
Wollastonite	15.0
EPK	20.0
Talc	6.0
Silica	<u>19.0</u>
Total	100.0

Comments:
1. Copper leaching with 5% copper carbonate, 5% rutile and 8% Zircopax: 5.3 mg/l

Unity Formula

Fluxes
K_2O	0.075
Na_2O	0.140
CaO	0.624
MgO	0.161
ZnO	

Stabilizers
Al_2O_3	0.357
B_2O_3	0.211
Fe_2O_3	0.004

Glass Formers
SiO_2	3.276
TiO_2	0.002
Si:Al	9.2:1

A Zinc Semimatte/Glossy Base Glaze

High zinc glazes were originally developed during the period when substitutes for lead were being sought. The Bristol glazes, developed in the 19th century in Bristol, England, are the most famous of zinc-containing glazes and were used from temperatures of about 1150-1300°C. Cone 6, of course, is well within that range.

Zinc glazes, however, have some problems and they are used only occasionally today with boron-fluxed glazes having largely replaced them. Their deficiencies include 1) a tendency to crawl 2) a tendency to pinhole and 3) the "muddying" of some colors. The tendency to pinhole is probably due to localized reduction of zinc oxide to zinc metal—yes, localized reduction can occur in an electric kiln—and making sure you have some airflow through your kiln can often minimize pinholing. This is one case where a kiln exhaust system is not just a safety feature, but it can improve the quality of your finished product.

Zinc also has some unique and desirable characteristics. It can be both a flux and an opacifier at the same time, particularly above about 0.3 molar equivalents. Some very nice translucent glazes can result. Bristol-type glazes can have a very nice satin surface. Zinc also gives attractive blues and greens from cobalt and copper respectively.

Our zinc-containing glaze below is within the general range of composition for Bristol glazes, although zinc is at the upper end of its normal range.

> This is the first recipe in this book containing a large amount of nepheline syenite. While it is an excellent source of sodium and potassium fluxes, it has the well-deserved reputation of causing glazes to "hardpan" in the bottom of the bucket. The secret to avoiding this is to make sure your nepheline syenite containing glazes have at least 10% clay in them. While this particular recipe settles more than some, it did not hardpan in our tests. If it does for you add 1-2% bentonite.

Zinc Semimatte/Glossy Base Glaze

Glaze Recipe		Unity Formula	
		Fluxes	
Nepheline Syenite	36.0	K_2O	0.059
Wollastonite	13.0	Na_2O	0.189
Zinc Oxide	10.0	CaO	0.332
EPK	10.0	MgO	0.020
Silica	<u>31.0</u>	ZnO	0.401
Total	100.0		
		Stabilizers	
Comments:		Al_2O_3	0.394
1. Copper leaching with 5%		B_2O_3	
copper carbonate and 6%		Fe_2O_3	0.003
rutile: 1.82 mg/l			
		Glass Formers	
		SiO_2	3.482
		TiO_2	0.001
		Si:Al	8.8:1

> The expansion/contraction characteristics of this glaze are very similar to those of the medium/low glaze in Chapter 5. It should fit most Cone 6 clay bodies well.

Stoneware and Porcelain Glazes

This glaze changes in surface character more than most depending on the specific colorants and opacifiers. With no additives it is a nice semiopaque satin or semimatte. With, for example, 5% copper carbonate and 5% rutile it is quite glossy.

In Figure 6-17 below, notice how well **Light Stormy Blue** breaks off texture. We were also intrigued by the huge effect rutile has on this glaze as illustrated in Figures 6-18 through 6-22 on the following pages. As you can see this might be a fascinating glaze to explore more extensively with colorant and opacifier variants. We will leave that exploration to the reader.

While all of our glazes have been developed in the oxidizing atmosphere of an electric kiln, **it is particularly important that this glaze be used only in oxidation.** Zinc is easily reduced to zinc metal, which is quite volatile at normal glaze firing temperatures. If reduced it will easily vaporize not only changing the character of the glaze, but also depositing zinc compounds on the surrounding area. Since this glaze contains a significant amount of zinc, this recommendation is particularly important.

> Zinc oxide has the reputation of lumping up during storage and being almost impossible to use. Both authors have had bags of zinc oxide in their studio for years without this happening. The secret: we keep our glaze materials dry! Always store your materials in sealed plastic bags or boxes, not in the paper bags in which they often are packaged for sale.

Figure 6-17. **Light Stormy Blue** *on tan stoneware. Zinc Semi-matte/Glossy Base Glaze with 1.0% cobalt carbonate and 4.5% rutile. Leach testing for cobalt was done on another color variant shown on the next page.*

MASTERING CONE 6 GLAZES

Figure 6-18 (left). **Smash It Before It Multiplies Blue.** *Zinc Semimatte/Glossy Base Glaze with 1% cobalt carbonate.*

Figure 6-19. **Midnight Blue.** *Zinc Semimatte/Glossy Base with 1.0% cobalt carbonate and 1.5% rutile.*

Figure 6-20 (left). **It Was a Dark and Stormy Night Blue.** *Zinc Semimatte/Glossy Base with 1.0% cobalt carbonate and 3.0% rutile.*

Figure 6-21. **Light Stormy Blue.** *Zinc Semimatte Glossy Base with 1.0% cobalt carbonate, 4.5% rutile.*

Stoneware and Porcelain Glazes

Figure 6-22. **Caribbean Sea Green**. *Zinc Semimatte/Glossy Base with 1.0% cobalt carbonate, 6.0% rutile. Leaching of cobalt: <0.02 mg/l.*

Specialty Glazes

As noted in the introduction to this chapter, specialty glazes are those that are quite stable with the particular colorants/opacifiers illustrated below; however they do not quite meet our standards for a base glaze that is more broadly useful. If you want to experiment with other colors, be particularly thorough in your testing of these glazes.

A Chrome/Tin Pink Glossy Glaze

It is well known that chromium oxide and tin oxide, combined in the same glaze, will give a pink color that ranges from a barely discernible blushing to a deep pink cranberry or raspberry color. Most such glazes at cone 6 have relied on Gerstley Borate as their source of boron and on some of the "magical" impurities in Gerstley Borate to bring out the maximum color in this type of glaze. We have even heard it said that you couldn't get a nice deep pink in a non-Gerstley Borate glaze. We beg to differ! The glaze below, named **Raspberry**, is an outstanding example of a Chrome/Tin Pink. It is smooth and glossy and very attractive. It is very similar to some of the darker types of reduction copper reds.

Don't think, however, that you can make an even deeper color by significantly increasing the chromium oxide level. If you do you may well end up with the ugliest green glaze you have ever seen. If you are disposed to experiment with different colorant levels we recommend you work between 0.1 and 0.5% chromium oxide.

> This glaze has the highest expansion/contraction characteristics of any of our glazes–almost as high as the medium expansion glaze in Chapter 5. While we have not seen any crazing over a period of several months on the clay bodies we used, we suspect it might eventually craze on our stoneware bodies.

Raspberry

Glaze Recipe		Unity Formula	
Whiting	20.0	*Fluxes*	
Nepheline Syenite	18.0	K_2O	0.035
Ferro Frit 3134	14.0	Na_2O	0.165
OM-4 Ball Clay	18.0	CaO	0.791
Silica	30.0	MgO	0.011
Total	100.0	ZnO	
Add:			
Green Chrome Oxide	0.2	*Stabilizers*	
Tin Oxide	7.5	Al_2O_3	0.285
		B_2O_3	0.147
Comments:		Fe_2O_3	0.005
1. Chromium leaching: <0.02 mg/l			
		Glass Formers	
		SiO_2	3.025
		TiO_2	0.009
		Si:Al	10.6:1

Stoneware and Porcelain Glazes

While this glaze leaches no measurable amount of chromium it does show a slight loss of gloss (but no loss of color) in the accelerated simmering sodium carbonate dishwashing test described in Chapter 3. Use your own judgement on whether or not you put it on pots likely to go in the dishwasher regularly.

This glaze can be applied without too much concern over getting a smooth coating—it levels itself out well. It also breaks nicely off of texture or edges as you can see in Figure 6-23.

*Figure 6-23. **Raspberry**. Recipe on the facing page. Leaching of chromium: < 0.02 mg/l.*

Waxwing Brown

When you adjust glaze composition to have a very high ratio of silica to alumina you can get some unusual effects. Glazes similar to the one on this page have appeared in the open literature, usually with Gerstley Borate as a significant ingredient. They have also often achieved the high Si/Al ratio with a "normal" level of silica and an unusually low level of alumina. While this results in a very attractive glaze it also yields one of questionable stability. In developing this glaze we have used frits rather than Gerstley Borate as our source of boron, we have kept alumina level at the minimum we recommend in Chapter 4 (0.25) and have increased the silica to get a Si/Al ratio of greater than 15.

We speculate that this glaze is separating into 2 different glassy phases with different things happening in each phase. When it is applied thickly it is a very attractive, but more uniform, Cedar Waxwing Brown. When applied thinly it can show some very spectacular crystals, which give it a more varied appearance. Note that with this particular glaze base recipe we have not been successful in developing other colors with this attractive a coloration pattern. This glaze, as presented with red iron oxide as a colorant, is very stable to acid leaching. It will also survive 30 cycles in a dishwasher with no problem. It does not do so well in the accelerated dishwasher test using simmering sodium carbonate solution (Chapter 3). Some loss of gloss and color is seen. We suggest it not be used on dinnerware. If you decide to use it with other colorants please test the resulting glazes thoroughly. Notice how this glaze breaks off edges giving a very nice accent with very little difference in appearance between stoneware and porcelain (Figures 6-24 and 6-26). It also does well on texture as the tile in Figure 6-25 shows.

The **Waxwing Brown** base has the lowest expansion of any of our glazes—even lower than the Low expansion glaze of Chapter 5. Adding iron oxide brings the expansion up to a level where it should fit most Cone 6 bodies. Do not, however, use this glaze without colorant as a liner glaze. Doing that would surely take you into a range where dunting or shivering is likely.

Waxwing Brown

Glaze Recipe		Unity Formula	
Ferro Frit 3134	34.5	*Fluxes*	
Talc	9.5	K_2O	0.010
OM-4 Ball clay	25.0	Na_2O	0.215
Silica	<u>31.0</u>	CaO	0.508
Total	100.0	MgO	0.267
Add:		*Stabilizers*	
Red Iron Oxide	15.0	Al_2O_3	0.251
Titanium Dioxide	1.5	B_2O_3	0.419
		Fe_2O_3	0.007
		Glass Formers	
Comments:		SiO_2	4.013
1. Iron leaching: 1.03 mg/l		TiO_2	0.014
		Si:Al	16.0:1

Stoneware and Porcelain Glazes

Figure 6-24. **Waxwing Brown** *on a stoneware sake jar. Recipe on the facing page.*

Figure 6-25 (left). A 4-inch by 4-inch (10 cm X 10 cm) stoneware tile with a single dip of **Waxwing Brown.** *This is an excellent glaze for highlighting texture.*

Figure 6-26. **Waxwing Brown** *on a porcelain sake jar. Note that it still breaks to dark brown or black over the texture and the edges of the pot.*

105

Waterfall Brown

While we were experimenting with Waxwing Brown, we took an excursion into the realm of high boron glazes—significantly above what traditional limit formulas would suggest. We found what is perhaps the most stunning cone 6 glaze either of us has ever seen. For this glaze we increased (silica + boron)/Al ratio to 15.7. With the boron level at 0.77, this glaze does a lot of moving. It is very fluid at cone 6.

In fact we would offer our readers a challenge. Consider this glaze to be your final exam in glaze craftsmanship. If you can mix, apply and fire this glaze and consistently get results similar to ours, you are a very skilled in applying glazes. This glaze needs to be applied at a thin to medium thickness, preferably medium at the top of the pot tapering to thinner at the bottom. This will let the glaze do some moving without running off the pot. If you get it on too thick you will get the opportunity to grind glaze off your kiln shelves. It is also strictly for use on stoneware. The higher level of flux in a porcelain body will interact with the glaze and cause it to run even more than it does on stoneware. On porcelain it is almost certain you will get to grind shelves. Believe us—we know from experience!

Again this is a specialty glaze that is quite stable in its own right, but the base does not meet our copper leaching criteria. It does, however, pass our more rigorous dishwasher test so it should be a good glaze to use on dinnerware. We have shown our Waterfall glaze only in brown, but have experimented with different colors. So far both the blue and green

> This glaze is similar in expansion/contraction characteristics to Waxwing Brown. With the iron oxide it should not be a problem; however without the iron it may well shiver or cause dunting.

Waterfall Brown

Glaze Recipe	
Ferro Frit 3134	33.5
Ferro Frit 3195	26.0
OM-4 Ball Cay	17.0
Silica	<u>23.5</u>
Total	100.0
Add:	
Red Iron Oxide	12.5
Rutile	1.0

Comments:
1. Iron leaching: 0.127 mg/l

Unity Formula	
Fluxes	
K_2O	0.007
Na_2O	0.319
CaO	0.664
MgO	0.010
Stabilizers	
Al_2O_3	0.298
B_2O_3	0.772
Fe_2O_3	0.004
Glass Formers	
SiO_2	3.917
TiO_2	0.010
Si:Al	13.1:1

versions, while also spectacular, are showing some small blisters, which we find unacceptable. We have not seen this fault in **Waterfall Brown**. We hope you will enjoy the challenge of this beautiful glaze.

Figure 6-27. ***Waterfall Brown*** *on a stoneware sake jar. This is not a glaze to be used on porcelain.*

A Cone 6 "Maiolica" Glaze

Maiolica (my-ol-ica) or majolica (ma-joe-lica), ah, the debates we potters can have. We have decided to go with the definitions provided by Hamer and Hamer (pages 207-209), which seem well researched. They define maiolica as decorated tin-glazed earthenware and majolica as a late 19th century ware with shiny colorful glazes. Of course we are not going to use tin or earthenware so it would probably be most accurate to call this glaze a "faux-maiolica" glaze.

Whatever we call it, more and more practitioners of the art of maiolica are moving up to cone 6 from the traditional earthenware clays and firing temperatures. They also like the relative economics of the opacifier zirconium silicate vs those of the traditional opacifier, tin oxide. The maiolica glaze shown below is designed to meet those needs. Its origin goes back several years to a workshop Ron Roy was leading. One of the objectives undertaken in that workshop was development of such a glaze and this was one of the top candidates that emerged. It is derived from a recipe originally developed by Linda Blossom.

One word of caution on doing maiolica on functional ware—we can only provide a good stable base glaze. We have no way to predict whether or not the stains you use for your brushwork on the surface of this glaze will leach badly or not. Only you can determine that by thoroughly testing your final product. We do recommend, however, that you use this same glaze without the added zirconium silicate as the base for your colorants. That is what we

> This glaze has an expansion coefficient which should result in it fitting most cone 6 bodies.

Ron's Cone 6 "Maiolica" Glaze

Glaze Recipe		Unity Formula	
Nepheline Syenite	23.0	*Fluxes*	
Ferro Frit 3124	23.0	K_2O	0.050
Whiting	14.0	Na_2O	0.218
EPK	17.0	CaO	0.725
Silica	<u>23.0</u>	MgO	0.007
Total	100.0		
Add:		*Stabilizers*	
Zircopax	16.0	Al_2O_3	0.502
		B_2O_3	0.165
		Fe_2O_3	0.004
Comments:			
1. Not leach tested. Contains nothing of concern		*Glass Formers*	
		SiO_2	3.497
		TiO_2	0.002
		Si:Al	6.96:1

Stoneware and Porcelain Glazes

have done on the piece shown in Figure 6-28. Also we highly recommend you limit your decorative work to the outside of functional pieces.

Figure 6-28. Ron's Cone 6 "Maiolica" Glaze on a porcelain jar. The brushwork was done with same base glaze minus the Zircopax. 7.5% of Dark Green and Cobalt Aluminate stains were added.

Alumina and Magnesia Matte Glazes

Developing alumina and magnesia matte glazes that meet our stability and reliability criteria has not been successful. Alumina mattes generally begin to form at Si/Al ratios of less than 5.0 but 4.0 or less is even better. If we use a silica level of 3.0 this means we will have to have an alumina level of approximately 0.75. This would be an extremely difficult glaze to melt at cone 6. Adding some boron can help, but if you add too much, you lose the matte surface. All of the dozen or so variants of alumina mattes we tried had leaching levels at least twice what we have set as our goals. Although we could easily specify an alumina matte that will hold low levels of colorants, we decided to focus our attention on our other glaze candidates and let this one go. While we haven't tried to make this type of glaze at cone 10, we believe we may fail there also. It could well be that as the aluminum-containing crystals form they are forming as alumino-silicates thereby pulling silica out the main melt and making formation of a glaze as stable as we are shooting for impossible. We will leave those experiments for a later time.

We have developed a magnesia matte that is very stable; however it is not a reliable glaze. It is right on the edge of crawling and is just too sensitive to application thickness and firing conditions. Again, more experiments for another time.

Summary

We hope you find our glazes useful and attractive and that you are able to reproduce them with minimal trouble. It is the authors' opinion that a number of them are so attractive you will have your gas-firing reduction friends looking them over very closely and asking how you got a "reduction" glaze out of your electric kiln. We hope these glazes are only starting points for you. There is a whole world of color and opacity variants to be explored within the framework of the base glazes described above. Please regard the specific base glazes we show as good places to start in your own exploration of glazes.

When you have explored these to your own satisfaction, then begin developing your very own glazes as we discuss in the next chapter. There are still an infinite number of stable and attractive glazes to be found; we have barely scratched the surface with the glazes in this chapter.

7
DEVELOPING YOUR OWN GLAZES

Developing your own glazes is a lot of fun and, frankly, most potters get a lot of satisfaction from having their very own special glaze. We encourage you to develop your own glazes and, in this chapter, will try to show you some efficient ways to do so.

Many potters use the "follow your nose" technique for glaze development. That is, they try a recipe they got from someone else. When they don't like the results (which they usually don't it seems) they fiddle with it hoping to get something better. If, after a couple of tries, they don't get something they like they move on to another recipe and start over. This is a very inefficient method for developing glazes.

Instead we would ask you to visualize the glaze you want in your mind. Is it glossy, semiglossy, satin or matte? Is it transparent, translucent or opaque? Is it solid color or variegated or mottled? What color is it? Write these characteristics down. Now you have something to work with. Let's work our way through them one at a time.

Glossy versus Matte

Within the domain of stable glazes it is easier to make or find glossy glazes than mattes or semimattes. As a general rule, glazes with multiple fluxes and a silica-to-alumina ratio of 7 or higher will be glossy assuming they are well melted during firing. To make semimattes and mattes you have to push the ends of the normal ranges. For example, you can make a high calcia matte or semimatte, but the calcia level has to be greater than 0.8 and preferably close to 0.9 in Seger unity formula terms. You also normally work at lower silica-to-alumina of 5-7 when you want matte glazes.

Alumina mattes can be made when silica/alumina ratios are 5 or less, preferably about 4.0. This means if you are aiming at a silica level of 3.0 the alumina level must be about 0.75. This is well above the normal range for alumina. On the other hand if alumina is kept in a more normal range, there will not be enough silica to make a stable glaze. As we discussed in the preceding chapter, we have not been able to make an alumina matte that meets our stability goals

High strontia mattes and semimattes, which can be very attractive, can also be made. Here there is a little more flexibility to use high levels of soda and potash because strontia has a low expansion coefficient and will offset the expansion of soda and potash.

Magnesium can also be used at levels of 0.3-0.5 in the Seger unity formula to make a matte or semimatte. However magnesium mattes are tricky. If you use too much you can have very low expansion and an increased tendency to crawl. If you use too little, of course, you will not get the nice buttery surface that magnesia is noted for. The range of 0.3-0.4 is probably the best place to search at Cone 6.

So if you want to develop a glossy glaze, start with a good mix of fluxes (including boron) combined with a silica level of at least 3.0 and an alumina level of 0.35-0.40. If you want to develop a semimatte or matte, start with high levels of calcia, strontia or magnesia. Again, keep your silica level at 3.0 or above and combine that with an alumina level of, say, 0.4 or a little higher. Use just enough boron to get your glaze thoroughly melted. Remember, these are just approximations. Good glossy and matte glazes can be made outside these ranges, but staying within these parameters will make the job easier when you are new to glaze formulation.

Level of Transparency/Opacity

The level of transparency or opacity is determined primarily by the level of opacifiers (zirconium, tin or titanium based compounds) added to glaze. However, matte and semimatte glazes are inherently more opaque than glossy glazes because the matteness is the result of tiny crystals present in the fired glazes. These same crystals will increase opacity as well as matte the surface of the glaze. The level of colorants also affects the opacity with higher colorant levels reducing transparency.

If you want a transparent glaze, focus on glossy or semiglossy glazes having no opacifiers and moderate levels of colorants. If you want an opaque glaze you can use either glossy or matte glaze bases and assure opacity by adding appropriate levels of opacifiers.

Solid Color versus Variegated Glazes

The specific color you are seeking is often a significant factor in choosing a starting point. For example, if you want pure blue you should avoid the use of magnesium as magnesium and cobalt often result in a mauve or purple color. Similarly chrome and tin will often give pink—which is nice if that's what you want and to be avoided if you don't want it. A good reference for helping you get to the right colors is *The Potter's Palette* by Constant and Ogden.

With functional glazes, we are limited in the amount of variegation we can tolerate. Certainly variegation of color is fine, but variegation of surface evenness is probably off-limits except, for example, on the outside of vases or jugs. Therefore we will ignore techniques like creating localized craters with the aid of silicon carbide. In fact we will focus on only one material:

titanium dioxide or the ore, rutile, which contains a high percentage of titanium dioxide. Titanium dioxide is well known for its ability to cause color variegation or mottling and using up to 10% of it in a glaze may help give your glaze that type of visual interest. As shown earlier in Chapter 4, modest amounts of rutile can also improve glaze durability.

With that preliminary discussion of setting goals for the glaze you want to develop, we will now diverge and describe two separate glaze development approaches. While the authors agree on a most things, we take different approaches when developing glazes.

Ron's Approach to Glaze Development

As a clay and glaze consultant to two clay suppliers I am called upon to "fix" glazes practically every day. I need to be able to cure the problems a potter encounters. Using the molecular approach I can usually do this.

If one has a reasonable knowledge of the specific qualities that each oxide brings to a glaze the solution is rather easy—providing you can keep your eye on all the different aspects and implications of what changes you are making.

The most common problems are substituting for materials that are not locally available or have been discontinued. Using the molecular approach is particularly appropriate when one material is replaced with another. The only requirement is to have a percent analysis for each material entered into your glaze calculation program.

I am often asked to develop glazes for individuals. It is then necessary that I know what is required and I can usually solve the problem by either making a glaze from scratch or starting with a glaze that has some of the properties needed.

Actually any glaze I begin with is good enough—all I need is a starting point. Some of the criteria might be as follows:

The glaze must:

- Melt well at Cone 6 but not run.

- Not craze or shiver.

- Resist marking and scratching.

- Give bright coloration with red iron oxide.

- Be durable when used as a liner.

- Be semi transparent and semi gloss.

From the above description I know certain oxides are not appropriate—zinc oxide is inconsistent with bright coloration from red iron oxide. Otherwise I can use what I want, consistent with the customer's supply.

I also know that there are certain recommended molecular limits for a cone 6 glaze. I use these as guidelines along with ratio and calculated expansion to help anticipate what the melted glaze will look like.

The logic involved is not complicated—if you were making icing for a cake you would have some of the same problems. You would understand what to do if the icing was too thin. If a glaze is too fluid when melted, i.e. it runs off the pot, you would know or would be able to find out which oxides promote running and which slow it down. It then becomes a matter of decreasing the runners and/or of increasing those that slow running down.

I don't say it is easy or simple—I do say that most of us can learn to do it. That is especially the case if we have models of glazes that do work to help us understand.

This book is mostly about durable glazes. You have many models of excellent glazes here—they mostly tell you how much silica and alumina is needed in a well-melted glaze for it to be stable. This means you have the examples you need to make other durable glazes, assess other glazes, and improve your present glazes using the molecular approach.

You can substitute other materials, change melting and fit attributes, substitute oxides for better color response and improve durability. There is one qualification—you need glaze calculation software and the knowledge to use it.

Example Recipe 1

Glaze Recipe		Unity Formula	
G-200 Feldspar	22.0	Fluxes	
Ferro Frit 3134	18.0	K_2O	0.080
Talc	13.0	Na_2O	0.120
Whiting	9.0	CaO	0.520
EPK	20.0	MgO	0.290
Silica	18.0	Li_2O	
		ZnO	
		BaO	
		Stabilizers	
Comments:		Al_2O_3	0.330
1. Not smoothing out well; small pits and pinholes.		B_2O_3	0.180
		Glass Formers	
2. Calculated Expansion = 434.37		SiO_2	2.810
		Si:Al	8.4:1

Let's take a simple example—a potter is having trouble because a glaze is not smoothing out well in the cooler part of the kiln and in fact there are some small pits and pinholes. The recipe and corresponding Seger unity formula being used is shown in Example 1.

I can't tell much about this glaze by just looking at the recipe; however, the molecular formula tells me a lot. I know that those oxides that make a glaze stiff are MgO and Al_2O_3 and those that are at the opposite end of the viscosity list are K_2O and Na_2O. I know that the expansion is right for many cone 6 bodies, and I also know it has enough silica and alumina to be durable. Therefore I need to replace some of the MgO with sodium and potassium (K_2O and Na_2O). The easiest way to do this is by increasing the level of feldspar; however if I use more spar I will increase the expansion and the glaze may start to craze. I need to rethink. Another way would be to use more frit—it has some sodium—and the B_2O_3 has a very low expansion to help balance it—let's see what happens.

Example Recipe 1–First Revision

Glaze Recipe
G-200 Feldspar	21.5
Ferro Frit 3134	22.0
Talc	12.0
Whiting	7.5
EPK	20.0
Silica	17.0

Comments:
1. Not smoothing out well; small pits and pinholes.
2. Calculated Expansion = 438.25

Unity Formula

Fluxes
K_2O	0.070
Na_2O	0.140
CaO	0.520
MgO	0.270
Li_2O	
ZnO	
BaO	

Stabilizers
Al_2O_3	0.330
B_2O_3	0.220

Glass Formers
SiO_2	2.840
Si:Al	8.5:1

If we compare the recipes we can't make much sense of what I have done but the molecular story is much more revealing:

• CaO is the same.

• MgO is down a bit—good because it's partly responsible for the pinholes and the lack of smoothing out.

• K_2O is down but the Na_2O is up by two—good that helps the flow.

• B_2O_3 is up—that's good because it helps the melt.

- Al_2O_3 is the same—we will try lowering that on the next try if we need to.

- SiO_2—about the same—good—it's needed for durability.

- Si/Al Ratio—the same—good that means the surface will be the same or close.

- Expansion is almost the same—good.

I would do a second glaze with less alumina—just to make sure the problem was solved in the shortest time. In the end, a combination of using the molecular formula and line blending is the shortest route to modifying and creating glazes. When we see the results of our experiments we can see what the effects of the oxides are on a glaze. That gives a much more instructive picture than trying to surmise the effect of different materials, most of which are complex collections of many oxides. Some portions of these materials are lost during firing (LOI—loss on ignition) which further complicates the picture. Calculation programs take this into account.

John's Approach to Glaze Development

I have evolved my glaze development technique by integrating several characteristics I have found or believe to be true about glazes.

First, I follow the four "rules" for formulating stable glazes; however, I often go outside the guidelines. While staying within the guidelines might maximize my chances of making a stable glaze, I find those glazes are often less interesting than those outside the guidelines.

Second, I believe that the volumetric line blending technique has merit in certain situations. While I use this technique, I practice it in a very different way than is recommended by Currie when incorporated into his grid method. For a functional potter, the grid method results in many unstable glazes with no easy way to sort the good from the bad. It is probable that of the 35 glazes in a typical 5 x 7 grid only 5-10 will be sufficiently stable to be of interest to a functional potter. I find that linear volumetric line blends almost always meet my needs for defining a good base glaze composition.

Third, I have come to conclude that if you blend two durable glazes, the result will almost certainly be a durable glaze. Certainly "Rules" 1 and 2 will still be intact if both glazes met those rules. "Rule" 3 will probably still be met because you will nearly always be increasing the number of fluxes and that will result in either a lower melting point or the same as one of the two original glazes. So while I don't have enough data to be certain I will get a durable glaze by blending two durable glazes, I think the odds are extremely high.

Therefore, when I want a glaze containing a high level of magnesia to get that buttery surface for which magnesia is known I will go through the following steps:

1. Pick a glaze with which I am familiar and that has a satin surface but which contains no magnesia. I might use one of the high calcium semi-mattes we presented in Chapter 6.

2. Design a new glaze, following the 4 "rules" which contains as much magnesia as possible (say 0.5-0.6). In designing this glaze I will keep the silica/alumina ratio about the same as in the glaze I picked above. I'll also choose the rest of the fluxes plus boron so that I think it has a good chance of melting as well as having a coefficient of thermal expansion in the range I want. This choice comes mainly from experience.

3. I'll add 5% copper carbonate and 6% rutile to both glazes and mix 500 grams of each. This will result in five 200 gram batches which is enough to dip one or more test tiles in each and get good coverage. I'll dilute each batch to the same volume using a graduated cylinder. For purposes of illustration and to keep the numbers simple, lets say each of the two batches is 750 ml for a total of 1500 ml. I know that to make a 5-part line blend I need to divide each glaze into 10 parts as shown in the table below.

Sample	A	B	C	D	E
Parts of Glaze 1	4	3	2	1	0
Parts of Glaze 2	0	1	2	3	4
ml of Glaze 1	300	225	150	75	0
ml of Glaze 2	0	75	150	225	300

Table 7-1. An example of volumetric line blending

Now I use a calibrated syringe to measure the appropriate amount of each glaze into 5 separate containers and I end up with 300 ml of each of my 5 line blend samples. This is enough to coat a couple of test tiles—one stoneware and one porcelain—plus coat the inside of a test cup for leach testing. After firing I will first vinegar test the coupons and visually examine each glaze in the line blend to narrow down my leach testing.

If one or more of the samples which has the surface I want and meets my leach testing goals, I will begin to experiment with various colorants with that base glaze. If not, I'll make appropriate adjustments and try again—sometimes doing another line blend and sometimes just one or two variations of something that is close. Working this way I always know that I will have candidates that have relatively good stability. They may not meet the criteria for a general purpose base glaze we described in Chapter 6, but they will very likely be useful as specialty glazes over a more limited color range. I don't have to spend time with glazes that are very attractive but are so unstable that they perform like the glazes we showed in Chapter 1.

I will sometimes use a 5 x 5 grid with the same base glaze in each corner for color development. For example if I want to explore muted blues, I might put 1% cobalt carbonate and 6% rutile in all 4 corner glazes. Then in one corner I will put nothing additional. In another corner, 3% copper carbonate. In the third corner, 0.2% nickel oxide and in the forth corner 1.0% nickel oxide. This will give me colors from a medium cobalt blue to a blue-green to a gray green. For the detailed procedure of mixing glazes for a grid experiment see Currie's book.

Figure 7-1. Good record-keeping is very important to effective glaze development.

Good record keeping is key in my approach to glaze development. I prefer to use a bound notebook that has pages large enough to paste a full 8 1/2 x 11 sheet of paper on each page. This method has several advantages over file cards or other methods. First you are assured of a chronological record of your test work. Second, it is much harder to misplace a research notebook than a file card or single piece of paper. Third, by numbering pages you can cross reference your test results back to the original experiment so you can easily find things in the future. Because of my research background, I use notebooks specifically designed for the purpose of keeping research records, but any bound notebook would be just as good.

Summary

Formulating your own glazes can be exciting and fun. At the same time you can carry this pursuit too far and never settle on and really learn how to use your best glaze or glazes. We believe the key is a disciplined rather than a random approach. Whether you use a glaze development methodology similar to the approaches described here or something entirely different, design your approach with care and then use it consistently. And do keep good records in a way that keeps them safe over the years. Doing that will save you a lot of repeated experiments and keep you from losing important information.

Bibliography

Bailey, Michael and Hewitt, David, "Calculating Crazing", *Ceramic Review*, No. 113, 1988

Constant, Christine and Ogden, Steve, *The Potter's Palette*, Radnor, PA: Chilton Book Company, 1996.

Cooper, Emanuel and Royle, Derek, *Glazes for the Potter,* New York: Charles Scribner's Sons, 1978.

Currie, Ian, *Revealing Glazes: Using the Grid Method*, Maryvale, Australia: Bootstrap Press, 2000.

Eppler, Richard A. and Eppler, Douglas R., *Glazes and Glass Coatings*, Westerville, OH: The American Ceramic Society, 2000.

Fournier, Robert, *Illustrated Dictionary of Practical Pottery,* Revised Edition, New York: Van Nostrand Reinhold Company, Inc., 1977.

Green, David, *Pottery Glazes,* New York: Watson-Guptill Publications, 1973.

Hamer, Frank and Hamer, Janet, *The Potter's Dictionary of Materials and Techniques*, 3rd edition, London: A & C Black, 1991.

Hopper, Robin, *The Ceramic Spectrum*, 2nd edition, Iola, WI: Krause Publications, 2001.

McKee, Charles, *Ceramics Handbook,* Belmont, CA: Star Publishing Company, 1984.

Pinnell, Pete, "Adjusting Glazes for Application", Parts 1 and 2. *Clay Times*, March/April and May/June 1998.

Pitelka, Vince, *Clay, A Studio Handbook,* Westerville, Ohio: The American Ceramic Society, 2001.

Rhodes, Daniel, *Clay and Glazes for the Potter*, revised and expanded by Hopper, Robin, 3rd edition, Iola, WI: Krause Publications, 2000.

Rossol, Monona, "Respirators and Dust Masks", Parts 1 and 2, *Clay Times*, Nov/Dec 1999 and Jan/Feb 2000.

Sax, N. Irving, *Dangerous Properties of Industrial Materials,* 6th edition, New York: Van Nostrand Reinhold Company, 1984.

Taylor, J.R. and Bull, A.C., *Ceramics Glaze Technology*, Oxford: Pergamon Press, 1986.

Zakin, Richard, *Ceramics, Mastering the Craft,* Radnor, PA: Chilton Book Company, 1990.

Glossary

Note: This glossary is a potter's glossary. The terms defined may well have other meanings in other fields. For a far more complete discussion of these terms and many others see Hamer and Hamer or Fournier.

A

Acetic acid: CH_3COOH. Used to test acid stability of glazes, usually at a 4 volume per cent level. Note that regular white or cider vinegar usually contains 5% acetic acid and is useful for in-studio testing.

Alkali: In potter's terms, these are non-coloring metal oxides that serve as fluxes in a glaze; specifically, lithium oxide (Li_2O), sodium oxide (Na_2O) and potassium oxide (K_2O).

Alkaline earth: These are non-coloring oxides which also serve as fluxes in glazes. Compared to the alkalis they are less soluble in water and, hence, are easier to use in glazes. However, they are less active fluxes and give less bright color responses. They include beryllium oxide (BeO), magnesium oxide (MgO), calcium oxide (CaO), strontium oxide (SrO) and barium oxide (BaO). Potters often include zinc oxide (ZnO) in this category; although that is not a technically accurate categorization.

B

Ball Clay: A secondary clay (one which has been moved from the geographical location where it was formed by forces of nature) characterized by high plasticity and a low to moderate level of impurities such as iron oxide and carbonaceous matter. Ball clays have good green strength and they usually fire to a cream color. Ball clays always have more silica and less alumina than kaolins.

Baria: Barium oxide.

Beryllia: Beryllium oxide.

C

Calcia: Calcium oxide.

Calcium carbonate: $CaCO_3$ or whiting. Make sure to buy this product from your pottery supplier and ask for an analysis. The product sold as lime or limestone at your garden store may be calcium carbonate or dolomite or something in-between.

Copper carbonate: While we use the notation $CuCO_3$ in this book, the material potters know as copper carbonate is really the mineral malachite and, technically, is more correctly known as cupric carbonate. Its chemical formula is $Cu(OH)_2 \bullet CuCO_3$

Crawling: A glaze defect where the glaze separates during drying and/or sintering and leaves an area that is bare of glaze.

Crazing: A glaze defect that results when the glaze is "too small" for the body. Said another way, the glaze contracts more than the body during cooling and the resulting stresses cause the glaze to form a network of cracks. This is an undesirable defect on functional pottery; however, it is often done purposefully for decorative effect on nonfunctional work.

Cristobalite: One of the crystalline phases of silica which is of particular interest to potters because it undergoes a sharp 3% expansion/contraction at 226°C (439°F). Note that this temperature is within the range achievable in a home oven. An excess of cristobalite in a clay body can cause dunting or shivering. Cristobalite is very rarely a problem at Cone 6.

D

Dilatometer: A device used to measure thermal coefficients of expansion and contraction. See Chapter 5 for more detail.

Dunting: Cracking of pottery caused by stresses, which build up during heating or cooling. Can occur either with bisque or glazed ware. Often caused by too rapid or uneven cooling, excess free silica in the clay body or poor glaze/body fit. Dunting of glazed ware always occurs when the glaze has solidified and, therefore, dunting cracks have sharp edges.

Durability: In this book we use the term durability to encompass all the properties necessary to have a long-lasting, relatively inert functional glaze. We use stability interchangeably with durability.

E

Epsom salts: Hydrated magnesium sulfate. Epsom salts can flocculate a glaze thereby making it thicker. If glazes are properly formulated and mixed, they shouldn't need the addition of Epsom salts. Occasionally, however, it can be a useful aid.

F

Feldspar: A group of minerals containing alkalis, alumina and silica. They can be considered to be natural frits or glazes. By themselves, though, they don't have all the properties we want in a glaze and, therefore, are only used as part of a total glaze recipe. They are usually subdivided into sodium and potassium feldspars depending on which is present in higher proportions. Of the feldspars we use in the recipes in this book, both Custer and G-200 are potassium feldspars. F-4 is an example of sodium feldspar.

Flint: Silica containing less than 5% impurity. Usually the terms silica and flint are used interchangeably—impurities are usually minimal in the materials available to potters in North America. If you see a recipe developed in Europe that specifies flint in a significant amount, you need to be careful in substituting silica for flint one-to-one.

Flocculation: The altering of the physical nature of a suspension of particles so the individual particles aggregate into larger particles. Glazes which do not promptly "dry" when applied to the surface of a pot can benefit from flocculation. This results in fewer, larger particles in the suspended glaze, which don't plug the pores in the clay surface. The net result is that the water in the glaze slurry will be free to absorb into the clay more readily and the glaze will "dry" and can be handled sooner. If the glaze is too deflocculated, the tiny particles will plug the pores in the clay surface and prevent further absorption of water. The result is a glazed surface that stays "wet" for a long period of time. Epsom salts is a common flocculant. It is, however, also possible for a glaze that is over-flocculated to dry slowly on the bisque surface. This happens because the glaze has become so thick that a lot of water has been added to bring it back to working consistency. This additional water can't be completely absorbed by the bisque surface and the glaze stays "wet" for a long time. It is seemingly contradictory phenomena like these that make flocculation and deflocculation so confusing.

Flux: An oxide that promotes melting in a ceramic mixture when it interacts with other oxides.

Frit: A manufactured mixture of materials that has been compounded to contain specific amounts of fluxes, alumina and silica. Frits are very uniform in composition and, therefore, are very reliable glaze materials. Frits also allow easier incorporation of soluble materials such as boron, sodium and potassium into a glaze recipe. Frits have a disadvantage in that they are sometimes difficult to keep in suspension in a glaze slurry.

G

Gerstley Borate: A boron-containing mineral that is no longer mined. It was both treasured and hated by potters because of its variable composition. It is a variant of colemanite.

Glass-former: For potter's purposes there are only 2 glass-formers of primary interest: silicon dioxide and boric oxide. These are materials that retain their amorphous (noncrystalline) molten state as they cool and become solids. One important difference between boron and silica is that boron never recrystallizes on cooling while silica can, if given enough time.

H

I

Iron Oxide: A compound of iron and oxygen. Two chemical forms are available to potters: red iron oxide (Fe_2O_3) and black iron oxide (FeO). Within these two chemical forms there are several purity levels. The most common (and that which we have used in our glaze recipes) is red iron oxide. In oxidation firing, Fe_2O_3 is the normal final state of the iron regardless of the starting state and the resulting color is a shade of brown or red-brown. In reduction, however, iron compounds can give colors such as gray-green (celadon), black, or red-brown depending on the timing and degree of reduction used during the firing cycle. Iron is a strong flux in reduction.

J

K

Kaolin: Kaolin is a primary clay (one that is usually found where it was formed). It has lower plasticity than ball clays (secondary clays) but also has fewer impurities. It always has more alumina and less silica than ball clay

L

Lime: Calcia or calcium oxide. To gardeners, lime is calcium carbonate or whiting, although if you buy lime in a garden supply store you may get dolomite.

Lithia: Lithium oxide.

LOI: Loss on ignition. A measure of the weight percent of the material that is lost during firing—primarily a representation of water and carbonaceous content of the material. Burning off of these materials takes time and is one of the reasons we recommend slow firing cycles.

M

Magnesia: Magnesium oxide.

Maiolica: Decorated tin-glazed earthenware.

Malachite: See copper carbonate.

Manganese Dioxide: A metal oxide used as a colorant in glazes. It primarily gives browns and blacks, but it can also give violet in glazes high in alkalis and low in alumina. Handle this product with extreme care. Inhalation of dust or fumes can cause very serious health problems.

N

Nepheline Syenite: A feldspathic mineral (technically, not a feldspar but a first cousin) of the formula $K_2O \bullet 3Na_2O \bullet 4Al_2O_3 \bullet 8SiO_2$. It is an excellent source of soda in glaze recipes. Because it contains sodium, part of which is soluble, it can deflocculate glazes and clay bodies if enough is present.

Nickel Oxide: A general name for the compounds of nickel and oxygen. Generally available to potters as black or green nickel oxide which both have the same chemical composition of NiO with the color difference being due to impurities. In a glaze, it usually results in gray color at levels of less than 3%.

O

Ochre: An iron oxide ore sometimes used by potters as a source of iron. Also sometimes applied to clays having a very high iron content. Ochre has a variable composition.

Opacifiers: A mineral which, when included in a glaze recipe, makes the glaze partially or completely opaque. The most popular opacifier today is zirconium silicate because of its reasonable cost; however, tin oxide and titanium dioxide are also used. In glazes such as a high calcium matte, crystals of calcium silicate act as an opacifier.

P

Potash: Potassium oxide.

Petalite: A feldspathic mineral containing lithium. An insoluble source of lithium. Sometimes difficult to obtain and expensive. Spodumene is usually a more economical source of lithium.

Pinhole: A tiny smooth-edged hole in a fired glaze surface. Gas bubbles that work their way up through the molten glaze and burst cause pinholes. Slow firing and soaking at peak temperature can give pinholes time to heal over. Firing to a higher bisque temperature can help, thereby getting rid of more volatile material before glaze is introduced. Also using materials like wollastonite as a source of calcium instead of whiting results in less evolution of gas during firing. Pinholing is more of a problem with higher viscosity glazes such as those which contain a significant amount of magnesium or aluminum.

Q

Quartz: One of the crystalline phases of silica—the one nearly always found in nature.

R

S

Seger: Herman Augustus Seger is the father of modern glaze chemistry. He did his important work in the last half of the 19th century. Potters perhaps best know him for the Seger Unity Formula (see Appendix B) and for the invention of pyrometric cones, but he also made numerous other contributions to ceramic science.

Silica: Silicon dioxide (SiO_2). The most common form available to potters is called quartz or flint. The primary glass-former in a glaze. Other forms of silica of interest to potters are amorphous silica and cristobalite.

Soda: Sodium oxide.

Soda Ash: Sodium carbonate ($Na_2Co_3 \cdot 10\ H_2O$). Also called washing soda. Occasionally used as a glaze component, although its solubility in water causes problems. Useful in testing durability of glazes to alkaline conditions.

Shivering: A glaze defect that occurs when the glaze is "too big" for the body, i.e. when the body contracts more than the glaze during cooling. Said another way, the coefficient of expansion of the glaze is too low when compared to that of the body. Shivering is a dangerous condition that can result in sharp splinters of glaze flaking off a pot resulting in cut fingers or tongues and angry customers—don't even think about what might happen if a splinter of glaze gets into a person's digestive tract.

Stability: See durability.

Strontia: Strontium oxide.

Superpax: A trade name for zirconium silicate. Other materials having a similar composition are Zircopax, Opax and Ultrox. All have about the same opacifying performance.

T

U

Ultrox. See Superpax.

V

Vents. Potters usually use this term in reference to electric kiln vent systems, which are highly desirable safety features and also serve to assure an oxidizing atmosphere in the kiln. They usually consist of a small blower and ductwork attached to the bottom of the kiln and leading out through the building wall.

X

Y

Z

Zircon: Zirconium silicate ($ZrO_2 \cdot SiO_2$). See Superpax.

Zirconia: Zirconium dioxide (ZrO_2). A glaze opacifier.

Zircopax: A trade name for a product that is about 95% zirconium silicate. Used as a glaze opacifier and converts to zirconia during firing.

Postscript

We have had a lot of fun writing this book. We hope you can tell that we feel deeply about the issues of good craftsmanship and making durable glazes that fit well and hold up well in use. We plan to continue working in this general area and, as we said in the Preface, consider this to be a "work in progress". We invite your participation. We are always open to constructive suggestions on how to improve this book or areas for additional research. To this end we have inaugurated a web site,

htttp://www.masteringglazes.com

where we will periodically update our progress and report your progress as well. Over time we would like to see this web site become a useful resource for potters who want to make good functional glazes. For example, if you are using a material specific to your location and have obtained a good analysis for it we will be happy to post the composition of that material on our site so others may have access to it. If you have leach tested a glaze and want to share your results with others we will also post that. Just send us as much information as you can about the source of your material analysis or the name of the lab that leach tested your work. We welcome any information you care to send that will be of use to others. We will add a form to the web site that will make sending us information easy to do. You can also send it by email to:

info@masteringglazes.com

While we are closing the text with the writing of this page, we urge you to look through the Appendices that follow. They also contain lots of information which we believe will help you on your journey to making beautiful and high quality glazes.

John and Ron

Appendices

A

RECOMMENDED MATERIALS

The following materials are those we have found to be readily available in North America. They also are relatively stable in composition from batch to batch. Although most of these materials contain several oxides, we have chosen to list them by their primary use.

Caution: Many of these material are hazardous either because they contain free silica or because they are toxic in their own right. Learn about them and take appropriate safety precautions before using them. Always ask your supplier for a Material Safety Data Sheet (MSDS) when you buy a new material and keep those MSDS sheets near at hand.

There are two materials in the following lists whose potential hazard goes beyond the warnings in the above paragraph. Nickel oxide is on the National Institute of Health (NIH) list as "reasonably anticipated to be a human carcinogen". For more information visit the NIH site at www.nih.gov/ Extended inhalation of manganese-containing dust and/or fumes is known to result in chronic manganese poisoning. Symptoms can resemble those of Parkinson's Disease. For more information see Sax Dangerous Properties of Industrial Materials. Both materials can be handled safely, but know what you are doing.

Primary Sources of Fluxes

G-200 Feldspar

Custer Feldspar

Nepheline Syenite

F-4 Soda Feldspar

Cornwall Stone

Whiting

Dolomite

Talc

Bone Ash or tricalcium phosphate

Wollastonite

Spodumene

Petalite

Strontium Carbonate

Magnesium Carbonate

Zinc Oxide

Ferro Frit 3110

Primary Sources of Boron

Cadycal

Ferro Frit 3124

Ferro Frit 3134

Ferro Frit 3195

Ferro Frit 3269

Ferro Frit 3278

Fusion Frit F12

Primary Sources of Alumina

EPK

Bell Dark

Kentucky OM-4

Ferro Frit 3292

Primary Sources of Silica

Silica (or Flint or Quartz)

Colorants, Opacifiers and Processing Additives

Bentonite

Zircopax

Superpax

Rutile

Titanium Dioxide

Tin Oxide

Red Iron Oxide

Cobalt Carbonate

Copper Carbonate

Chromium Oxide

Nickel Oxide (see cautionary note at beginning of this Appendix)

Manganese Dioxide (see cautionary note at beginning of this Appendix)

Materials that are Specifically NOT Recommended

Lithium Carbonate—Too soluble and difficult to control. Can lead to very serious shivering and, in some cases, crazing on the same pot. Levels under 2% are usually OK.

Barium Carbonate—Toxicity concerns

All Lead and Cadmium containing materials–Toxicity concerns

Gerstley Borate—Very nonuniform and questionable future availability

Colemanite—Very nonuniform and expensive when available.

Cryolite—Used for making blisters and craters in a glaze–not a desirable characteristics in functional glazes.

B

THE SEGER UNITY FORMULA

Background

In the late 1800s, Herman Seger developed a way of thinking about glaze composition that is still relevant today. A brief discussion and illustration of this technique follows.

Seger divided the components of a glaze into 3 categories of materials: 1) modifiers or fluxes, more correctly called basic oxides. These are the materials that lower a melting point of a glaze. 2) stabilizers, more correctly called amphoteric or trivalent oxides. Stabilizers, particularly alumina, raise a glaze's viscosity when melted and keep it from running off vertical surfaces on a pot. 3) glass formers, more correctly called acidic oxides. Glass formers do exactly what the name implies.

Table B-1 shows the oxides, which are used in this book, by category. For simplicity we will stay with the terms fluxes, stabilizers and glass formers and leave the more correct terms for the ceramic scientists.

Fluxes	Stabilizers	Glass Formers
Sodium Oxide – Na_2O	Aluminum Oxide (Alumina) – Al_2O_3	Silicon Dioxide (Silica) – SiO_2
Potassium Oxide – K_2O	Boric Oxide – B_2O_3	
Lithium Oxide – Li_2O	Iron Oxide — Fe_2O_3	
Calcium Oxide – CaO		
Magnesium Oxide – MgO		
Zinc Oxide – ZnO		
Strontium Oxide — SrO		

Table B-1. The oxides of materials used in glazes, by category.

Like all things in life, the classification of these oxides into the categories is not as simple as we would like and the above chart represents an oversimplification that requires some explanation. First, to repeat, only the oxides used in this book are shown; a more complete list would include things such as lead, fluorine and others. Second, the metals used as colorants and opacifiers – such as copper, cobalt, manganese, chromium, tin, titanium and zirconium – are not shown because they generally are not thought to interact in a meaningful way with the glaze chemistry. Rather, they can be regarded to be physical residents in "holes" in the glaze matrix and they do not need to be considered when studying the basic glaze chemistry. This is not a totally accurate picture; however it is adequate for our needs.

Another complication is the role of boron. While traditionally treated as a stabilizer, it has properties that could place it in all three categories. It is a glass former and it also serves to lower the melting point of a glaze, thereby serving the role of a flux. In some of the early literature on glaze research arguments rage back and forth about the proper categorization of boron. Today, mostly as a matter of tradition and the fact that boron is trivalent like aluminum, it is always treated as a stabilizer in glaze calculations. One must be aware of its multiple roles to do an optimum job of glaze formulation.

After Seger divided glaze components into three categories, he devised a standard way to calculate the relative amounts of each component in the glaze recipe that remain in the fired glaze. This is important to restate: Seger showed us how to look at the composition of the fired glaze based on the input materials. He first took the weight percentages of each material (minerals, frits or specific inorganic compounds) in the glaze and converted those to molar equivalents of each by dividing the percentage of each by its molecular weight. To do this you must know the molecular composition of each mineral or glaze component so molecular weights can be calculated. The second step was to convert these molar equivalents calculated for each mineral to molar equivalents of each relevant oxide. Now he had the relative number of molecules or moles of each of the oxides in Table 1 expressed as a molar equivalent. The third step was to convert these molar equivalents to molar percentages. His fourth and final step is what gives the Seger unity formula its name. He arbitrarily decided to set the sum of the molar fractions of the fluxes to be equal to 1.0. This is a step that could be called normalizing and has the effect of allowing one glaze to be compared to another very easily.

A Simple Example

Table B-2 shows a brief illustration of these steps for a very simple glaze recipe, without going through the details of the calculations. The glaze

Table B-2. The steps required to convert a glaze recipe to a Seger unity formula.

Glaze Recipe (1)		Molar Equivalents of each Mineral (2)	Molar Equivalents of the Relevant Oxides (3)		Molar Percentages of the Oxides (4)	Unity Formula (5)
Potassium Feldspar	70	0.126	K_2O	0.126	9.16	0.386
Whiting	20	0.200	CaO	0.200	14.55	0.614
Flint	10	0.167	—			
			Total Fluxes	0.326	23.71	1.000
			Al_2O_3	0.126	9.16	0.386
			SiO_2	0.923	67.13	2.831
			Total	1.375	100.00	

recipe on the left is converted to the molar equivalents of each mineral in the second column. The third column shows the molar equivalents of each relevant oxide in the minerals; the fourth column gives the molar percentages of each oxide; and the fifth column, the unity formula.

It is important to work through these calculations one time to understand where they come from; however, we highly recommend using one of the readily available computer programs to calculate them on a routine basis. The use of a computer to aid in this task will be discussed at the end of this chapter. Let's describe the calculations in more detail.

To get from the recipe weight percentages in Column 1 to the molar equivalents of each material in Column 2 you must know the molecular formula and molecular weight of each material. We are using theoretical compositions for this illustration to keep things simple; however, actual compositions are readily available for the materials of interest to potters whether they are minerals or man-made frits. An up-to-date list of the compositions of all the materials used in this book is in Appendix F.

Potassium feldspar has the theoretical molecular formula of:

$K_2O \bullet Al_2O_3 \bullet 6SiO_2$

and a molecular weight of 557.

Whiting or calcium carbonate has a molecular formula of:

$CaCO_3$

and a molecular weight of 100.

Flint or silica has the molecular formula of

SiO_2

and a molecular weight of 60.

The numbers in Column 2, then, are generated by dividing the numbers in Column 1 by the appropriate molecular weight, e.g. 70/557 = 0.126, 20/100 = 0.200 and 10/60 = 0.167.

The hard work is already done. From here on it is just a matter of some simple calculations. Note that each molecule of feldspar has 1 molecule of K_2O, 1 of Al_2O_3 and 6 of SiO_2. Each molecule of whiting or calcium carbonate will convert to 1 molecule of CaO upon firing. Of course, each mole of silica remains a mole of silica. To get from Column 2 to Column 3, multiply the molar equivalents of each mineral by the respective number of molecules of each oxide contained in that mineral. As an example, the number for SiO_2 in Column 3 is 6 times the molar equivalent of feldspar in Column 2 (because each molecule of feldspar contains 6 molecules of silica) plus the molar equivalents of silica itself.

(6 x 0.126) + 0.167 = 0.923

At the same time you are making these calculations, arrange the oxides in the order of fluxes, stabilizers and glass formers. If a particular oxide is contained in more than one mineral its molar equivalents must be summed.

To get from Column 3 to Column 4 you simply convert to percentages. Take the total of Column 3 (1.375); divide it into each of the individual numbers in Column 3 and multiply by 100. For example 0.126/1.375 times 100 equals 9.16% for alumina or Al_2O_3. Note that Column 4 now gives the oxide concentrations in the glaze as their molar percentages. As noted above, some people also find this a useful way to think about glaze compositions.

Finally, to get to the Seger Unity Formula in Column 5, you just normalize the fluxes, i.e. each number in Column 4 is divided by 23.71. There, we are done!

The Seger Unity Formula gives us a standardized way to think about glazes. If you will calculate the unity formula for every glaze you use and take time to look at the results you will soon find that it becomes a very convenient and useful way to display glaze composition. It also gives us a good way to communicate with each other when we are trying to understand why a particular glaze is behaving the way it does and what we might do to change that behavior. We will show the unity formula for every glaze in this book and use it repeatedly when we are describing a glaze's characteristics. If these last few paragraphs are still confusing to you, take some time to go over them again. A good understanding of this section will help immeasurably as you work through the rest of this book.

The Computer's Role in Glaze Formulation

As you can see from the preceding section, while doing unity calculations is simple in concept it can very quickly become quite complex and time consuming when the switch is made from the theoretical compositions that were used for illustration to real-life compositions of minerals and frits. Also, glazes usually contain several ingredients instead of the 2 used in the example above. This is a situation made for computers! Not only can a good computer program do the calculations in an instant, it can store the compositions of the materials we use as well as serve as a database for our personal collection of glaze recipes. Some of the available programs have added other features like calculating the thermal expansion of a glaze, calculating the cost of a glaze or maintaining an inventory of materials on hand.

If you own or have access to a personal computer, it will be well worth the time and money to invest in one of the available programs. They range from very inexpensive shareware programs that are based on a spreadsheet to fairly sophisticated commercial programs available from at least three sources around the world. They are available for Windows or Macintosh machines; however, not all programs are available for all machines. A summary of the programs we are aware of as we go to press is given in Appendix C. We highly recommend you obtain one of these programs if you plan to formulate your own glaze. While we don't recommend any one program over another, in selecting a program for your own use we suggest you examine things like:

1. Do the authors make support readily available. Ask them a question about their program and see how quickly and thoroughly they respond.

2. What programs are your friends using? It can be useful to compare results with them.

3. How regularly has the program been updated? Is it still being actively supported for your machine?

4. Is a trial version available that will allow you to test the program for a period of time before you buy it?

5. How flexible is the program? Can you easily add or modify the materials list? Does it meet your needs for a recipe database? Can you change the coefficients of expansion if needed?

Of course, price is important also and you will find a wide range of costs between the various programs we list in Appendix C; however, in our view cost should not be the primary consideration. You will find the program you choose will become more and more important to you as you learn to use it. If you plan to formulate your own glazes we believe having or having access to a glaze calculation program is extremely important.

C

PROGRAMS FOR GLAZE CALCULATION

There are computer programs available ranging from quite sophisticated to very basic. They are available for both Macintosh and Windows machines. What follows is simply a compilation of the programs of which we are aware and does not imply any recommendation on our part of one over another. Programs available only for Windows machines will usually run on a Macintosh that has Windows installed and switches between operating systems using Boot Camp, VMware Fusion or Parallels Desktop.

GlazeMaster™ by John Hesselberth

GlazeMaster is a glaze/clay calculation and database software program for both Windows and Macintosh machines. In Windows it runs on Windows 98 up to and including Windows Vista. On the Macintosh it runs on OS 8.6 - X. The OS X version runs on all versions of OS X (it has been thoroughly tested at this writing on versions 10.1 - 10.5.8. More information and fully functional 60-day trial downloads can be found on the internet at:

http://www.masteringglazes.com

or by mail at:

Frog Pond Pottery

P.O. Box 88

Pocopson, PA 19366-0088

USA

Phone: 1-610-388-1254

Fax: 1-610-340-2534

Insight by Tony Hansen and Digitalfire Corporation

Insight is available for Windows and Macintosh. Information can be found on the internet at:

http://www.digitalfire.com

or by mail/phone at:

Tony Hansen

1595 Southview Drive SE, Suite 407

Medicine Hat, Alberta

T1B 0A1 Canada

(406) 662-0136

HyperGlaze™ by Richard Burkett

HyperGlaze™, originally available only for the Macintosh has been rewritten and is now available for both Macs and Windows machines as well as Linux. Information can be found on the Internet at:

http://hyperglaze.com

or by mail at:

Richard Burkett

6354 Lorca Drive

San Diego, CA 92115

Matrix by Lawrence Ewing

Matrix is available for Windows machines. An earlier version for the Macintosh was available, but it is our understanding that there are no current plans to upgrade it. Information can be found on the Internet at:

http://www.matrix2000.co.nz

or by mail at:

Lawrence Ewing

1015 Ellis Road

Five Rivers, RD3 Lumsdem

North Southland

New Zealand

Email: lewing@woosh.co.nz

GlazeChem by Robert Wilts

GlazeChem is a shareware program for Windows; however at last report it did not work on Vista. Information can be found on the Internet at

http://www.glazechem.com/

or by mail at:

Robert Wilts

216B Main Street, Apt. 1B

Woburn, MA 01801

TESTING LABORATORIES FOR GLAZES

Nearly any laboratory that tests water for inorganic contaminants can test leachates from glazes for the materials we potters commonly use. However this is such a niche business that most labs are not interested. We are aware of only one laboratory that makes this service available at prices potters can afford. We have no financial interest in this laboratory.

Having your glazes tested is easy to do. Here are detailed instructions followed by information on the testing laboratory that was current as we went to press.

Having Glazes Tested for Extractable Metals

Having your glazes tested for extractable metals is quite easy and inexpensive. Here are the steps to follow:

1. Make a small cup. The cup can be most any size; however, some of us have agreed to a standard size to make our results more consistent and comparable. Unless you have a special reason to use a different size, we recommend you throw cups that are straight-walled cylinders 10 centimeters (4 inches) in diameter by 7.5 centimeters (3 inches) tall (wet dimensions). This size cup can be thrown from 400-450 grams (a little less than 1 pound) of clay by someone with modest throwing skills. An experienced thrower can probably do it with less than 400 grams of clay. Dry and bisque fire the cup, glaze it and glaze fire it at your standard conditions. Make sure the glaze completely coats the inside of the cup. It is best to put a pyrometric cone pack right next to the cup so you will know exactly what temperature (or more accurately, heat work) it saw during firing.

2. Call the laboratory (phone number below) to get their latest testing charges. At publication of this book, the cost is $18-20 to have one cup tested for one metal and $30-31 to have one cup tested for two metals.

3. Send the cup to:

Brandywine Science Center, Incorporated (BSC)

204 Line Road

Kennett Square, PA 19348

Phone: (610) 444-9850

4. Enclose a letter specifying what to test for and payment. There is an extra charge if you want your samples returned; call them directly to determine the charge. If you send multiple samples make sure they are well labeled so you will know which result goes with which sample.

5. In 1-3 weeks you will receive a written report on your glaze. BSC is certified by both Pennsylvania and Delaware environmental agencies. They have very helpful, friendly personnel.

An updated list of instructions on how to test your glazes can be found on the Internet at:

http://www.frogpondpottery.com/glazetest.html or at

http://www.masteringglazes.com/

E

FIRING CYCLES FOR ELECTRIC KILNS

As mentioned in Chapter 2, glaze firing of electric kilns is something to be studied and mastered just as with gas kilns. The big difference is that with gas kilns there is no choice—getting satisfactory results requires learning the nuances of your particular kiln. Electric kilns, on the other hand, can be fired simplistically. That is, you can turn the kiln switches on low for a couple hours, move them up to medium for a couple more hours and move them up to high until your Kiln Sitter® turns the kiln off. Ten to twenty hours later you open your kiln and unload. However, if you operate your kiln in this manner you are almost certainly not getting the best out of your glazes! Here are some guidelines we suggest:

1. Always raise temperature slowly until the kiln is at or slightly above 100°C (212°F). This is essential in bisque firing; however, it is also important in a glaze firing. Unevaporated water from the glaze slurry should be evaporated slowly. A good way to determine if all the water is gone is to open two spy holes so a natural draft is started (generally in the bottom hole and out the top hole). Hold a mirror or shiny piece of metal above the top spy hole. If it fogs there is still moisture present.

2. For bisque firings we recommend slow firing (100°C, 180°F per hour) from 100°C to 900°C (212F to 1650F). This is when chemically combined water and organics are burned off. This is especially important with iron bearing bodies to stop any reduction of iron which can over flux clay.

3. Temperature can then be raised as rapidly as desired until you approach within 100°C (180°F) of the end point whereupon you should again raise temperature slowly.

4. For bisque firing, a 5-10 minute soak at the end of the firing cycle can be advantageous. If the kiln is tightly packed it can help assure that each piece will be uniformly treated and, therefore, absorb glaze more evenly. For glaze firing, a 15-20 minute soak at peak temperature is very important. It is here that the glaze and the clay finalize their interaction with each other. They need time to do this.

5. For bisque firing, turning the kiln off and letting it cool naturally usually works fine. However, if you encounter any breakage of large pieces when you open a bisque kiln it may have been due to bisque dunting as the piece went through the quartz inversion temperature at 573°C (1063°F). This is

particularly a problem with porcelain which contains a significant amount of free silica. If you run into bisque dunting, slow down the cooling from 650 to 500°C (1202 to 932°F) and/or bisque to cone 04. For glaze firing, turning off a kiln and letting it cool naturally can be a disaster. For any glaze where you want multiple phases to develop (this can be crystals in a matte glaze or two glassy phases in some of the "floating" types of glazes or it can be a combination of both), slow cooling is essential. If you wish, you can drop rapidly away from peak temperature for the first 100-150°C (180-270°F). Cooling through the temperature range of 1025 down to 800°C (1900 down to 1500°F) should be controlled to no faster than 80°C per hour (approximately 150°F per hour). Your specific glazes may require conditions slightly different from these so we recommend you experiment to find your own best situation.

6. Below 800°C (1500°F), the kiln can be turned off and left to cool naturally.

The above recommendations make a strong case for having a high quality thermocouple or multiple thermocouples in your kiln (but not as a substitute for cones—always use large cones as your reference point) so you can assure the suggested temperature rise and fall rates. Of course the ideal situation is to have a computer-controlled kiln. If you do not have either, try turning you kiln switches to medium for about 4 hours after you reach peak temperature. By way of example, the author's computer cycles for glaze firing are shown in the table below.

Ramp No.	Temperature and Hold Time at the End of the Ramp		Rate of Temperature Increase or Decrease	
	°C/Hold	°F/Hold	°C/hour	°F/hour
1	105/0	220/0	55	100
2	1080/0	2000/0	200	350
3	1200/15	2190/15	85	150
4	1000/0	1900/0	-275	-500
5	760/0	1400/0	-70	-125

Notes:

1. Conversions between °C and °F are not necessarily exact; they have been rounded where exact temperatures are not important.
2. Hold times are in minutes.
3. Temperature rates are those programmed. In some cases the kiln may not be able to keep up.
4. Maximum temperature (1200°C/2190°F) is that required on author's kiln to reach Cone 6, tip touching. This is dependent on thermocouple calibration and age and should be adjusted as needed by each person. Cones are

Table E-1. An example of an electric kiln firing cycle that works for semimatte and matte glazes.

F

MATERIALS ANALYSES

Knowledge of the materials we use to make glazes is critical. Many of the materials we use are mined and the composition does change over time as the miners go farther and farther afield from the original starting point. While we have used materials that have a good reputation for stable composition over the years we nonetheless want to document the analyses we used in doing the Seger unity formula calculations for our glazes.

Like glaze recipes, materials analyses can be shown in multiple ways. The most common way is to show the composition by weight percentages of the individual oxides with a final number called the Loss on Ignition or LOI that represents the weight loss during firing. LOI primarily is a measure of the water and carbonate content prior to firing, although other things may be part of it also. It can also be useful to look at materials compositions as molar fractions (instead of weight fractions or percentages) and we do that also in the tables below by using Seger unity formula formats.

Here then are the materials for the glazes used in this book. Note that not all of the materials on our recommended list are included—only those that appear in our glaze recipes in Chapter 6.

Ferro Frit 3124

Material Analysis, weight %

SiO_2	55.3
Al_2O_3	9.9
B_2O_3	13.7
K_2O	0.7
Na_2O	6.3
CaO	14.1

Comments:

Unity Formula

Fluxes

K_2O	0.021
Na_2O	0.282
CaO	0.697
MgO	
ZnO	
BaO	

Stabilizers

Al_2O_3	0.269
B_2O_3	0.547

Glass Formers

SiO_2	2.557
Si:Al	9.5:1

Ferro Frit 3134

Material Analysis, weight %

SiO_2	46.5
Al_2O_3	
B_2O_3	23.1
K_2O	
Na_2O	10.3
CaO	20.1

Comments:

Unity Formula

Fluxes

K_2O	
Na_2O	0.317
CaO	0.683
MgO	
ZnO	
BaO	

Stabilizers

Al_2O_3	
B_2O_3	0.634

Glass Formers

SiO_2	1.476
Si:Al	

Ferro Frit 3195

Material Analysis, weight %

SiO_2	47.3
Al_2O_3	11.9
B_2O_3	23.5
K_2O	
Na_2O	6.2
CaO	10.9
MgO	0.12

Comments:

Unity Formula

Fluxes

K_2O	
Na_2O	0.336
CaO	0.654
MgO	0.010
ZnO	
BaO	

Stabilizers

Al_2O_3	0.392
B_2O_3	1.136

Glass Formers

SiO_2	2.656
Si:Al	6.7:1

Ferro Frit 3269

Material Analysis, weight %

SiO_2	49.7
Al_2O_3	13.2
B_2O_3	15.2
K_2O	8.1
Na_2O	11.1
CaO	0.1
ZnO	1.0
F	1.6

Comments:

Unity Formula

Fluxes

K_2O	0.306
Na_2O	0.641
CaO	0.009
MgO	
ZnO	0.044
BaO	

Stabilizers

Al_2O_3	0.462
B_2O_3	0.777

Glass Formers

SiO_2	2.955
Si:Al	6.4:1

Custer Feldspar

Material Analysis, weight %
SiO_2	69.02
Al_2O_3	17.13
B_2O_3	
Fe_2O_3	0.15
K_2O	10.08
Na_2O	3.02
CaO	0.30
LOI	0.30

Comments:

Unity Formula
Fluxes
K_2O	0.664
Na_2O	0.302
CaO	0.033
MgO	
ZnO	
BaO	

Stabilizers
Al_2O_3	1.043
B_2O_3	
Fe_2O_3	0.006

Glass Formers
SiO_2	7.142
Si:Al	6.8:1

G-200 Feldspar

Material Analysis, weight %
SiO_2	66.86
Al_2O_3	18.41
B_2O_3	
Fe_2O_3	0.08
K_2O	10.67
Na_2O	3.01
CaO	0.81
LOI	0.16

Comments:

Unity Formula
Fluxes
K_2O	0.643
Na_2O	0.275
CaO	0.082
MgO	
ZnO	
BaO	

Stabilizers
Al_2O_3	1.024
B_2O_3	
Fe_2O_3	0.003

Glass Formers
SiO_2	6.322
Si:Al	6.2:1

Nepheline Syenite

Material Analysis, weight %

SiO_2	60.70
Al_2O_3	23.30
B_2O_3	
Fe_2O_3	0.07
K_2O	4.60
Na_2O	9.80
CaO	0.70
MgO	0.10
LOI	0.70

Comments:

Unity Formula

Fluxes

K_2O	0.220
Na_2O	0.712
CaO	0.056
MgO	0.011
ZnO	
BaO	

Stabilizers

Al_2O_3	1.030
B_2O_3	
Fe_2O_3	0.002

Glass Formers

SiO_2	4.560
Si:Al	4.4:1

Talc
(Check for local variations)

Material Analysis, weight %

SiO_2	55.2
Al_2O_3	0.31
B_2O_3	
Fe_2O_3	0.16
K_2O	
Na_2O	0.34
CaO	8.42
MgO	30.0
LOI	5.41

Comments:

Unity Formula

Fluxes

K_2O	
Na_2O	0.006
CaO	0.167
MgO	0.827
ZnO	
BaO	

Stabilizers

Al_2O_3	0.003
B_2O_3	
Fe_2O_3	0.001

Glass Formers

SiO_2	1.022
Si:Al	309.6:1

Whiting
(Check for local variations)

Material Analysis, weight %		Unity Formula	
SiO_2	0.20	Fluxes	
Al_2O_3		K_2O	
B_2O_3		Na_2O	
Fe_2O_3	0.10	CaO	0.994
K_2O		MgO	0.006
Na_2O		ZnO	
CaO	55.10	BaO	
MgO	0.25	Stabilizers	
LOI	44.35	Al_2O_3	
		B_2O_3	
Comments:		Fe_2O_3	0.001
		Glass Formers	
		SiO_2	0.003
		Si:Al	

Wollastonite
(Check for local variations)

Material Analysis, weight %		Unity Formula	
SiO_2	51.91	Fluxes	
Al_2O_3	1.82	K_2O	
B_2O_3		Na_2O	0.005
Fe_2O_3	0.37	CaO	0.948
K_2O		MgO	0.047
Na_2O	0.27	ZnO	
CaO	42.10	BaO	
MgO	1.49	Stabilizers	
LOI	2.04	Al_2O_3	0.023
		B_2O_3	
Comments:		Fe_2O_3	0.003
		Glass Formers	
		SiO_2	1.093
		Si:Al	48.3:1

Zinc Oxide

Material Analysis, weight %
SiO_2
Al_2O_3
B_2O_3
Fe_2O_3
K_2O
Na_2O
CaO
ZnO   100.00
LOI

Comments:

Unity Formula
Fluxes
K_2O
Na_2O
CaO
MgO
ZnO   1.000
BaO
Stabilizers
Al_2O_3
B_2O_3
Fe_2O_3
Glass Formers
SiO_2
Si:Al

Edgar Plastic Kaolin (EPK)

Material Analysis, weight %
SiO_2 46.08
Al_2O_3 37.46
B_2O_3
Fe_2O_3 0.69
K_2O 0.40
Na_2O 0.04
CaO 0.13
MgO 0.12
TiO_2 0.30
P_2O_5 0.12
LOI   14.66

Comments:

Unity Formula
Fluxes
K_2O 0.417
Na_2O 0.063
CaO 0.227
MgO 0.292
ZnO
BaO
Stabilizers
Al_2O_3 36.050
B_2O_3
Fe_2O_3 0.423
Glass Formers
SiO_2 75.395
TiO_2 0.370
P_2O_5 0.083
Si:Al   2.1:1

MASTERING CONE 6 GLAZES

OM-4 Ball Clay

Material Analysis, weight %		Unity Formula	
SiO_2	55.20	**Fluxes**	
Al_2O_3	27.90	K_2O	0.345
B_2O_3		Na_2O	0.157
Fe_2O_3	1.10	CaO	0.174
K_2O	1.00	MgO	0.323
Na_2O	0.30	ZnO	
CaO	0.30	BaO	
MgO	0.40	**Stabilizers**	
TiO_2	1.20	Al_2O_3	8.902
LOI	12.6	B_2O_3	
		Fe_2O_3	0.224
Comments:		**Glass Formers**	
		SiO_2	29.941
		TiO_2	0.490
		Si:Al	3.4:1

Silica

It is normal practice to have the fluxes add to 1.000; however sometimes that isn't possible. In the case of silica there are no fluxing materials; therefore silica has been set to unity. It really makes no difference as the numbers in the unity formula are just ratios of the numbers of one oxide to another. In some displays of unity formulas for clays, you will see alumina set to unity and everything else is relative to that.

Material Analysis, weight %		Unity Formula	
SiO_2	99.80	**Fluxes**	
Al_2O_3	0.13	K_2O	
B_2O_3		Na_2O	
Fe_2O_3	0.06	CaO	
K_2O		MgO	
Na_2O		ZnO	
CaO		BaO	
LOI		**Stabilizers**	
		Al_2O_3	0.001
Comments:		B_2O_3	
		Fe_2O_3	0.001
		Glass Formers	
		SiO_2	1.000
		Si:Al	767.7

G

GLAZES USED FOR DEVELOPMENT OF RULES

Rule 1 (Have Enough Silica)

Silica Series–2.3

Glaze Recipe

G-200 Feldspar	24.5
Ferro Frit 3134	24.5
Wollastonite	12.3
EPK	24.5
Talc	14.1
Silica	0.0

Add:

Copper Carbonate	5.0
Zircopax	8.0
Rutile	5.0

Comments: Leaching of copper: 21.5 mg/l

Unity Formula

Fluxes

K_2O	0.074
Na_2O	0.135
CaO	0.505
MgO	0.287
Li_2O	
ZnO	
BaO	

Stabilizers

Al_2O_3	0.343
B_2O_3	0.208

Glass Formers

SiO_2	2.305
Si:Al	6.7:1

Silica Series–2.8

Glaze Recipe

G-200 Feldspar	22.0
Ferro Frit 3134	22.0
Wollastonite	11.0
EPK	22.0
Talc	12.7
Silica	10.4

Add:

Copper Carbonate	5.0
Zircopax	8.0
Rutile	5.0

Comments: Leaching of copper: 13.9 mg/l

Unity Formula

Fluxes

K_2O	0.074
Na_2O	0.136
CaO	0.504
MgO	0.286
Li_2O	
ZnO	
BaO	

Stabilizers

Al_2O_3	0.343
B_2O_3	0.207

Glass Formers

SiO_2	2.796
Si:Al	8.2:1

Silica Series–3.3

Glaze Recipe

G-200 Feldspar	20.0
Ferro Frit 3134	20.0
Wollastonite	10.0
EPK	20.0
Talc	11.5
Silica	18.5

Add:

Copper Carbonate	5.0
Zircopax	8.0
Rutile	5.0

Comments: Leaching of copper: 8.93 mg/l

Unity Formula

Fluxes

K_2O	0.075
Na_2O	0.134
CaO	0.505
MgO	0.287
Li_2O	
ZnO	
BaO	

Stabilizers

Al_2O_3	0.343
B_2O_3	0.206

Glass Formers

SiO_2	3.268
Si:Al	9.5:1

Silica Series–3.8

Glaze Recipe

G-200 Feldspar	18.1
Ferro Frit 3134	18.1
Wollastonite	9.1
EPK	18.1
Talc	10.4
Silica	26.2

Add:

Copper Carbonate	5.0
Zircopax	8.0
Rutile	5.0

Comments: Leaching of copper: 11.2 mg/l

Unity Formula

Fluxes

K_2O	0.075
Na_2O	0.134
CaO	0.503
MgO	0.288
Li_2O	
ZnO	
BaO	

Stabilizers

Al_2O_3	0.342
B_2O_3	0.205

Glass Formers

SiO_2	3.795
Si:Al	11.1:1

Silica Series–4.4

Glaze Recipe
G-200 Feldspar	16.4
Ferro Frit 3134	16.4
Wollastonite	8.2
EPK	16.3
Talc	9.4
Silica	33.3

Add:
Copper Carbonate	5.0
Zircopax	8.0
Rutile	5.0

Comments: Leaching of copper: 10.5 mg/l

Unity Formula

Fluxes
K_2O	0.076
Na_2O	0.133
CaO	0.504
MgO	0.288
Li_2O	
ZnO	
BaO	

Stabilizers
Al_2O_3	0.345
B_2O_3	0.205

Glass Formers
SiO_2	4.402
Si:Al	12.8:1

Rule 2 (Have Enough Alumina)

Alumina Series–0.13

Glaze Recipe
G-200 Feldspar	22.5
Ferro Frit 3134	22.5
Wollastonite	11.3
EPK	1.1
Talc	13.0
Silica	29.6

Add:
Copper Carbonate	5.0
Zircopax	5.0
Rutile	5.0

Comments: Leaching of copper: 23.7 mg/l

Unity Formula

Fluxes
K_2O	0.071
Na_2O	0.135
CaO	0.516
MgO	0.277
Li_2O	
ZnO	
BaO	

Stabilizers
Al_2O_3	0.129
B_2O_3	0.206

Glass Formers
SiO_2	3.137
Si:Al	24.3:1

Alumina Series–0.25

Glaze Recipe

G-200 Feldspar	21.1
Ferro Frit 3134	21.1
Wollastonite	10.5
EPK	12.0
Talc	12.1
Silica	23.2

Add:

Copper Carbonate	5.0
Zircopax	5.0
Rutile	5.0

Comments: Leaching of copper: 8.99 mg/l

Unity Formula

Fluxes

K_2O	0.074
Na_2O	0.135
CaO	0.515
MgO	0.276
Li_2O	
ZnO	
BaO	

Stabilizers

Al_2O_3	0.247
B_2O_3	0.206

Glass Formers

SiO_2	3.174
Si:Al	12.9:1

Alumina Series–0.34

Glaze Recipe

G-200 Feldspar	20.0
Ferro Frit 3134	20.0
Wollastonite	10.0
EPK	20.0
Talc	11.5
Silica	18.5

Add:

Copper Carbonate	5.0
Zircopax	5.0
Rutile	5.0

Comments: Leaching of copper: 5.31 mg/l

Unity Formula

Fluxes

K_2O	0.075
Na_2O	0.134
CaO	0.505
MgO	0.287
Li_2O	
ZnO	
BaO	

Stabilizers

Al_2O_3	0.343
B_2O_3	0.206

Glass Formers

SiO_2	3.268
Si:Al	9.5:1

Alumina Series–0.45

Glaze Recipe

G-200 Feldspar	19.0
Ferro Frit 3134	19.0
Wollastonite	9.5
EPK	28.5
Talc	10.9
Silica	13.1

Add:

Copper Carbonate	5.0
Zircopax	5.0
Rutile	5.0

Comments: Leaching of copper: 6.51 mg/l

Unity Formula

Fluxes

K_2O	0.074
Na_2O	0.135
CaO	0.513
MgO	0.277
Li_2O	
ZnO	
BaO	

Stabilizers

Al_2O_3	0.455
B_2O_3	0.203

Glass Formers

SiO_2	3.152
Si:Al	6.9:1

Alumina Series–0.55

Glaze Recipe

G-200 Feldspar	18.1
Ferro Frit 3134	18.1
Wollastonite	9.0
EPK	34.9
Talc	10.4
Silica	9.5

Add:

Copper Carbonate	5.0
Zircopax	5.0
Rutile	5.0

Comments: Leaching of copper: 14.0 mg/l

Unity Formula

Fluxes

K_2O	0.074
Na_2O	0.135
CaO	0.515
MgO	0.2776
Li_2O	
ZnO	
BaO	

Stabilizers

Al_2O_3	0.549
B_2O_3	0.202

Glass Formers

SiO_2	3.168
Si:Al	5.8:1

Rule 3 (Thoroughly Melt the Glaze)

Glaze A

Glaze Recipe
G-200 Feldspar	20.0
Ferro Frit 3134	20.0
Wollastonite	10.0
EPK	20.0
Talc	11.5
Silica	18.5

Add:
Copper Carbonate	5.0
Zircopax	5.0
Rutile	5.0

Comments: Leaching: See Figure 4-3.

Unity Formula

Fluxes
K_2O	0.074
Na_2O	0.135
CaO	0.513
MgO	0.277
Li_2O	
ZnO	
BaO	

Stabilizers
Al_2O_3	0.344
B_2O_3	0.203

Glass Formers
SiO_2	3.163
Si:Al	9.2:1

Glaze B

Glaze Recipe
Ferro Frit 3124	31.0
Wollastonite	23.2
EPK	31.7
Silica	14.1

Add:
Copper Carbonate	5.0
Rutile	5.0

Comments: Leaching: See Figure 4-3.

Unity Formula

Fluxes
K_2O	0.010
Na_2O	0.107
CaO	0.849
MgO	0.034
Li_2O	
ZnO	
BaO	

Stabilizers
Al_2O_3	0.507
B_2O_3	0.205

Glass Formers
SiO_2	3.235
Si:Al	6.4:1

Rule 4 (Use Moderate Levels of Colorants or Opacifiers)

The base glaze used for the Zircopax and rutile series was **Glossy Base Glaze 1** (See Chapter 6).

H

USEFUL REFERENCES FOR LEACHING DATA

Evaluation of leaching data is difficult, at best, given the lack of definitive knowledge on how much of the material leaching from a pot actually gets into food. In addition there is often very little knowledge of "how much is too much" with regard to various materials that might be ingested over a long period of time. Therefore we have assembled a list of what we call "useful references" that might give individual potters an indication of the relative toxicity of some of the materials we put in our glazes.

The following tables are not complete—they contain only materials likely to be of interest to potters. Nor are they intended, in any way, to be recommendations on what might be allowable levels of leaching. We maintain, as we stated early in this book, that a functional potter should avoid the most dangerous of materials (lead and cadmium) and then strive to make glazes at the very stable end of the glaze spectrum.

Lead and Cadmium Standards

Type of Tableware	FDA Maximum Leaching Levels for Lead, mg/l	California Prop. 65 Labeling Levels for Lead, mg/l	FDA Maximum Leaching Levels for Cadmium, mg/l
Flatware	3.0	0.226	0.5
Small Hollowware	2.0	0.1	0.5
Cups/Mugs	0.5	0.1	0.5
Large Hollowware	1.0	0.1	0.25
Pitchers	0.5	0.1	0.25

For definitions and more detail on the above table see FDA documents CPG 7117.06 and CPG 7117.07

Table H-1. A summary of lead and cadmium leaching standards in the U.S. and California.

Drinking Water Standards

U.S. Drinking Water Standards for Materials of Interest to Potters

Primary Standards (1)		Secondary Standards (2)	
Inorganic Contaminant	MCL in mg/l	Inorganic Contaminant	mg/l
Barium	2.0	Aluminum	0.05-0.2
Cadmium	0.005	Copper	1.0
Chromium	0.1	Iron	0.3
Copper	1.3	Manganese	0.05
Lead	0.015	Zinc	5.0
Nickel	0.1		

Notes:

(1) Maximum Contaminant Levels (MCL) are the maximum permissible levels of contaminant in water which is delivered to any user of a public water system.

(2) Secondary Standards are nonenforceable guidelines that may cause cosmetic or aesthetic effects.

Table H-2. Primary and secondary water standards for materials of interest to potters.

For more information on U.S. drinking water standards visit the EPA web site at:

http://www.epa.gov/safewater/mcl.html

There is also a "health advisory guideline" for boron in drinking water of 0.6 mg/l; however, there are no standards or useful references for some materials potters use which might be of interest (e.g. calcium, cobalt, lithium, magnesium, strontium, tin and titanium).

For a global perspective on water quality standards visit the World Health Organization web site at:

http://www.who.int/water_sanitation_health/index.html

or

http://www.who.int/water_sanitation_health/GDWQ/Summary_tables/Tab2a.htm

Recommended Daily Allowances and Vitamin Tablets

Of course, certain materials we use are actually required as part of our dietary intake. Information on recommended daily allowances can be found on the Food and Drug Administration site at

www.fda.gov/

Again, this is not in any way to recommend we should be providing dietary supplements with our pottery glazes, but rather to help those trying to gain a better understanding of the relative toxicity, or lack thereof, of some of the materials we work with.

Another source of information that some find useful is the composition of so-called "vitamin" tablets. For example, many multivitamins contain low levels of copper, iron, magnesium, calcium, manganese, zinc, chromium, potassium and nickel.

I

LIMIT FORMULAS FOR CONE 6 GLAZES

Over the years a number of authors have presented so-called "limit formulas". They published them with the clear disclaimer that they are only guidelines and that good glazes can be found outside of limits. As we pointed out in Chapter 4, limit formulas can be useful, particularly to help you find a balance of fluxes that is likely to provide good melting at the specified cone. Some authors, however, have not been as careful as others in providing limit formulas and have given sets of numbers that will clearly result in glazes which are not well melted or in ones that have less silica than needed. Rather than duplicate those limit formulas which we believe can result in nondurable glazes we have elected to show only two sets below: those provided by Cooper and Royle (p. 91) and those which the authors proposed in an earlier article in *Ceramics Monthly*. These two sets are very close to each other and are probably equally useful.

Oxide Range, Seger Molecular Formulas	Cooper and Royle	Hesselberth and Roy
$(K+Na)_2O$	0-0.375	0.1-0.3
CaO	0-0.55	0.2-0.6
MgO	0-0.325	0-0.3
BaO	0-0.4	
ZnO	0-0.3	0-0.2
SrO		0-0.2
Al_2O_3	0.275-0.65	0.25-0.5
B_2O_3	0-0.35	0-0.3
SiO_2	2.4-4.7	2.5-4.0

Table I-1. Limit formulas for Cone 6 glazes.

Index

A

acetic acid 121
alkali 121
alkaline earth oxides
   defined 121
   effect on stability 58
alumina
   importance of in stable glazes 53
   sources of 131
ASTM Standard Tests 43, 44, 45

B

Bailey, Michael 76, 119
balances
   calibrating and using 25
ball clay
   defined 121
barium carbonate 132
barium in glazes 14, 18
base glaze
   defined 84
Bell Dark 131
bentonite 131
bisque
   firing 30, 143
bisqueware
   cleaning 31
   waxing 31
bone ash 130
boron
   sources of 131
brushability of glazes 30
Bull, A.C. 120

C

cadmium 132
cadmium in glazes 14, 19
Cadycal 131
calcium carbonate 121
Cardew, Michael 22, 50, 82

chipping resistance. *See* testing glazes: chip resistance
chromium oxide 132
clay
   vitrification of 47, 68
clay/glaze fit
   defined 61
   determining 62–63
cobalt carbonate 132
colemanite 132
colorant levels
   importance for stability 55–56
   maximum recommended 56
colorants
   recommended 131
comparing glaze formulas 19–20
cone 6
   defined 85
   firing to 85
cones
   use of in firing 34
cones vs thermocouples 144
Constant, Christine 119
contraction. *See* expansion/contraction
   effect on clay/glaze fit 61
cooling rate of kilns
   35, 85, 86, <u>144</u>
Cooper, Emanuel 59, 119
copper carbonate 132
   defined 38, 122
copper in glazes 38
   bitter taste 15
Cornwall Stone 130
crawling
   defined 122
crazing
   defined 44, <u>61–62</u>, 122
   predicting 65, 73
   testing for 44–45
cristobalite
   defined 122
cryolite 132
Currie, Ian 116–117, 119

Custer feldspar 130, 148
cutlery marking test. *See* testing glazes: metal marking

D

deflocculation. *See* glaze deflocculation
   defined 123
dilatometer 122
   calibrating 74
   charts explained 63–67
   use described 63–66
dishwasher testing 43
dolomite 130
drinking water standards 160
dunting
   defined <u>62</u>, 122
   predicting 66
   testing for 44–45
durable glazes <u>14–17</u>, 18, 122. *See also* stable glazes, glaze stability
dust 23, 26
dust masks 23

E

EPK 131, 150
Eppler, R. A. and D. R. 56, 119
epsom salts 30, 122
expansion/contraction coefficients
   calculation of 70
   effect on clay/glaze fit 61–62
   interpreting 69–70
   measuring 63–66
   table of 76
   understanding units 69–70

F

F-4 soda feldspar 130
feldspar
   defined 123
Ferro frit 3110 131
Ferro frit 3124 131, 146
Ferro frit 3134 131, 146
Ferro frit 3195 131, 146
Ferro frit 3269 131, 146
Ferro frit 3278 131
Ferro frit 3292 131
firing
   bisque 30, <u>143–144</u>
   electric kilns 143
   glaze 34, <u>143</u>
   oxidation 85
   rate of temperature increase/decrease 35, <u>143</u>
   reduction 85
fit testing. *See* testing glazes: clay/glaze fit
fitting glazes to a clay body 61
flint
   defined 123
flocculation. *See* glaze flocculation
   defined 123
flux
   defined 123
   sources of 130, <u>133</u>
"food safe" glazes 14–17
Fournier, Robert 119
frit
   defined 123
functional pottery
   criteria for glazes 13
Fusion frit F12 131

G

G-200 feldspar 130, 148
Gerstley Borate 83, 132
   defined 124
glass formers
   sources of 133
glass-former
   defined 124
glaze
   base 84
   brushability 30
   liner 18
   specialty 84
glaze calculation programs
   list 138
Glaze Calculator 140
glaze calulation programs
   benefits of 136
   criteria for selecting 137
glaze chemicals
   analyses of 145
   mixing 24, 26
   not recommended 131
   purchasing 23
   recommended 130

safety of 130
storage 23
weighing 24
glaze deflocculation 28–30
glaze durability. *See* glaze stability
glaze firing 34
glaze flocculation 28–30
glaze materials. *See* glaze chemicals
glaze recipes
  Bone 89
  Bright Sky Blue 94
  Caribbean Sea Green 101
  Chrome/Tin Pink Glossy 102
  Clear Powder Blue 93
  Cone 6 "Maiolica" 108
  expansion test glazes 70
  Field Mouse Brown 87
  Glossy Base 1 92
  Glossy Base 2 96
  Glossy Liner Glaze 97
  High Calcium Semimatte Base 1 86–89
  High Calcium Semimatte Base 2 89
  It Was a Dark and Stormy Night Blue 100
  Licorice 96
  Light Stormy Blue 99
  Midnight Blue 100
  Oatmeal 87
  Powder Blue 93
  Raspberry 102
  Raw Sienna 89
  Ron Roy Black 96
  Smash It Before It Multiplies Blue 100
  Spearmint 89
  Variegated Blue 94
  Variegated Slate Blue 87
  Waterfall Brown 104
  Waxwing Brown 104
  Zinc Semimatte/Glossy Liner 98
glaze resist 31
Glaze Simulator 140
glaze stability
  alumina 53
  copper 38, 56
  effect of colorants 55–56
  effect of opacifiers 56–58
  flux balance 58–59
  melting 54–55
  overloading 55
  silica 52
Glaze Workbook 139
GlazeChem 139
glazes
  adjusting flocc/deflocc balance 29–30
  adjusting water level 26
  alumina mattes 110
  applying 32
  Bristol 98
  developing your own 111
  expansion test glazes 67–68
  gloss vs matte 111
  high Si/Al ratio 104–106
  magnesia mattes 110, 112
  maiolica/majolica 108
  melting of 65
  mixing 27
  opacity of 112
  predicting crazing 65
  problem solving 113–116
  rutile in 112
  sieving or screening 27
  softening point 64
  specialty 102
  strontium oxide in 111
  suspension of 28
  testing. *See* testing glazes
  "traveling" between potters 83
  variegation in 112
  zinc-containing 98–99
gloss vs matte surfaces 111
Green, David 33, 59, 119
grid method 116, 118

H

Hamer, Frank and Janet 20, 119
Hewitt, David 76, 119, <u>139</u>
Hopper, Robin 33, 119
HyperGlaze™ 138

I

ingredients. *See* glaze chemicals
Insight 138
iron oxide 124

K

kaolin
  defined 124
Kentucky OM-4 131
Kiln Sitter® 85
kilns
  firing 34, 143
  loading 34
  stacking 34

L

leach testing
  cost 141
  detectable limits 93
  instructions for 141
  interpretation of results 40–42
  professional laboratory
    40, 142
  resistance to acids 38–40
  resistance to bases 43
  with vinegar 39
leaching from glazes 42
leaching of lead and cadmium
  FDA standards 159
lead in glazes 14, 19, 132
lime
  defined 124
limit formulas
  examples of 162
  usefulness of 59–60
line blending 116–117
liner glaze 18
lithium (soluble) in glazes 18
lithium carbonate 132
LOI
  defined 124

M

magnesium carbonate 131
magnesium in glazes 112
malachite. *See* copper carbonate
manganese dioxide
  125, 130, 132
manganese poisoning 130
masks 23
materials analysis
  accuracy of 21

Matrix 139
matte vs glossy surfaces 111
McKee, Charles 59, 119
melting of glazes
  determination of 55
  importance for stability 54–55
metal marking
  testing for 46
microwave oven suitability
  testing for 47–48
molar percentages 19, 134
MSDS 11

N

nepheline syenite 130, 148
  defined 125
  use of in glazes 98
nickel oxide 125, 130, 132
notebook 118

O

ochre 125
Ogden, Steve 119
OM-4 ball clay 131, 152
opacifiers
  defined 125
  effect on stability 56–57
  sources of 131
opacity in glazes 112

P

petalite 125, 131
pinhole
  defined 125
Pinnell, Pete 29, 119
Pitelka, Vince 119
potter
  responsibility
    11, 17, 23, 42, 84

Q

quartz
  defined 126

R

record keeping 118

red iron oxide 131
responsibility of potter
    11, 17, 23, 42, 84
Rhodes, Daniel 20, 119
Rossol, Monona 119
Royle, Derek 59, 119
rules for stable/durable glazes
    52–54
rutile 131
    effect on stability 57–58
    in glazes 112

S

safety
    manganese dioxide 130
    nickel oxide 130
    overview 11, 23
    silica dust 23, 130
Sax, N. Irving 120
scales. *See* balances
scratch resistance test. *See* testing glazes: scratch resistance
Seger, Herman Augustus
    19, 51, 126, 133
Seger Unity formula 19–20, 133–136
    calculating 135
shivering
    defined 44, 62, 126
    predicting 66
    testing for 44–45
silica 131, 152
    crystalline form 64
    defined 126
    importance of in stable glazes
        52–53
soda ash
    for testing alkali resistance 43
specialty glaze
    defined 84
spodumene 130
stabilizers
    sources of 133
stable glazes 14–18, 18
    challenge test for 51
    formulating or making 51
storage of materials 24
strontium carbonate 131
strontium in glazes 111
Superpax 131

suspension of glazes. *See* glaze flocculation

T

talc 130, 148
Taylor, J.R 56, 120
testing clay
    vitrification 48
    water absorption 48
testing glazes
    chip resistance 47
    clay/glaze fit 44–45
    crazing or dunting 44–45
    metal marking 46
    microwave oven suitability
        47–48
    overview 37
    resistance to acids 38–40
    resistance to alkalis 43–44
    scratch resistance 46–47
    thermal shock 44–45
    with vinegar 39
thermocouples vs cones 144
tin oxide 131
titanium dioxide 131
transparency in glazes 112
tricalcium phosphate 130

U

unstable glaze
    illustration 15

V

variegation in glazes 112
vent systems 127
vinegar testing 39
vitrification
    testing clay for 48
volumetric line blend 116

W

water standards
    primary 41
    primary and secondary 160
waxing of bisqueware 31
weighing materials 24
weight percentages 19
whiting 130, 150

wollastonite 130, 150

Z

Zakin, Richard 33, 59, 120
zinc oxide 131, 150
 use of in glazes 99
zirconium silicate 127
 effect on stability 56–57
Zircopax 131

www.ingramcontent.com/pod-product-compliance
Lightning Source LLC
Chambersburg PA
CBHW041122300426
44113CB00002B/33